About the Book

There are 10 IGCSE Mathematics higher papers & answers in this book. These are 5 sets of papers 1 & 2 written as practice papers for IGCSE Mathematics Higher Examination in June 2021. Papers are mainly focusing on Edexcel examination board. However, you may still use this book as a practice for other International GCSE examinations as well as Edexcel.

These papers are written according to the new grade 9-1 syllabus and questions are potential questions for the upcoming IGCSE examination in June 2021. There have been only 5 examinations with this syllabus since June 2017. These 10 papers were written in a similar theme to those exams.

All the questions in this book are written by the author and they are new questions written purely to help and experience the students to prepare and test themselves for the upcoming mathematics IGCSE higher exams.

Answers, solutions and mark schemes are included in this book. If you need to check your solutions, I advise you to ask your school mathematics teacher or your private mathematics tutor to mark your answers.

There are 4 sections to this book A, B, C, D & E. Each section contains 2 papers. Both papers of each section are calculator papers.

International GCSE (IGCSE) Mathematics June 2021 Potential Papers

for the Edexcel grade 9 to 1 syllabus

Higher level

Includes 10 exam papers and answers

(can also be used as a revision guide for other exam boards)

By Dilan Wimalasena

Contents

Section A

IGCSE Mathematics
Paper 1
(calculator)

Potential Paper A1

June 2021

You must have: Ruler graduated in centimetres and millimetres, protractor, pair of compasses, pen, HB pencil, eraser.

Calculator is allowed

Time allowed
2 hours
Total 100 marks

Write answers to 3 significant figures unless stated otherwise

1. The points P & Q have coordinates $P(2,-3), Q(10,1)$.

   i) Work out the midpoint of PQ.

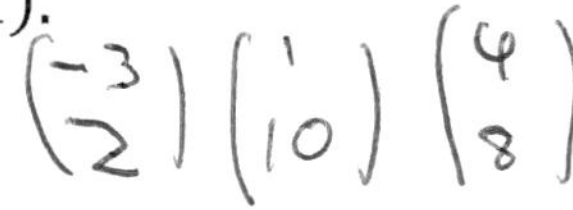

(2 marks)

   ii) Work out the gradient of the line PQ.

(2 marks)

   iii) Write down the perpendicular gradient to the line PQ.

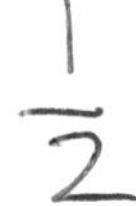

(1 marks)

   iv) Hence, or otherwise work out the equation of the perpendicular line to PQ through the midpoint of PQ.

(2 marks)
(total 7 marks)

2. Write 360 as a product of its prime factors.

(3 marks)

3. The circumference of a circle is 44cm. Work out its area.

(4 marks)

4. Below is a list of scores of 7 cricketers in a cricket match.

77, 81, 26, 7, 5, 19, 35

i) Work out the median score.

5, 7, 19, 26, 35, 77, 81 $\left(\frac{n+1}{2}\right) = 4$

(2 marks)

ii) Calculate the interquartile range.

$\frac{n+1}{4}$ $= 2$ 26

$\frac{3(n+1)}{4}$ $= 6$

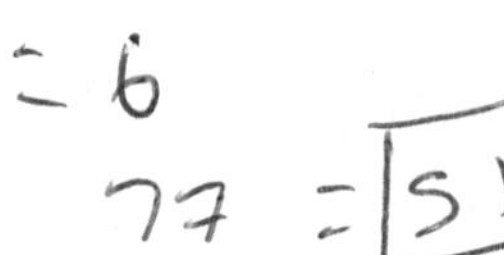

(3 marks)

iii) Draw a box plot.

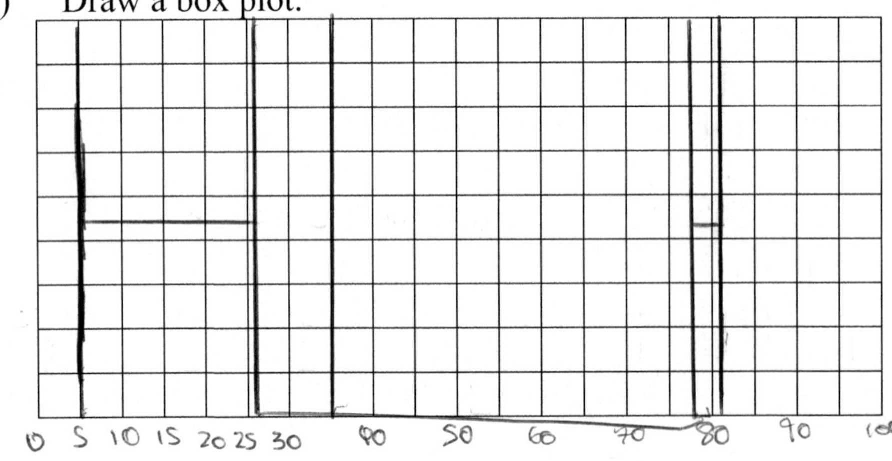

(2 marks)

(total 7 marks)

5. There were 2 red balls and 8 blue balls in a bag. Andrew took 2 blue balls out from the bag and replaced them with a red ball and a blue ball.

What is the probability of picking a red ball now?

$\frac{2}{10}$ R $\frac{8}{10}$ B

$\frac{2}{10}$ $\frac{6}{10}$

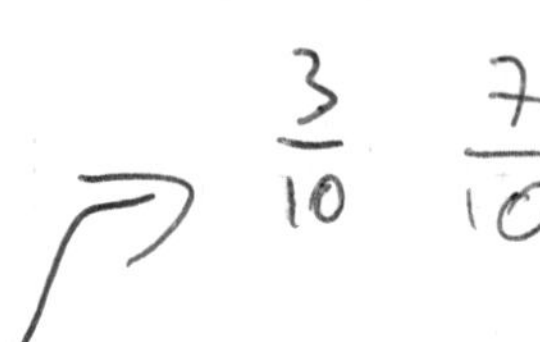

(3 marks)

6. Work out the following and write your answer in standard from.

$$(3.8 \times 10^{8}) \times (7.4 \times 10^{-6})$$

$380000000 \times 7.4 \times 10^{-6}$

$= 2812$

$= 2.812 \times 10^{3}$

(3 marks)

7. a) Expand and simplify.

$$(2x + 1)(x - 3)(x + 3)$$

FOIL

$(2x+1)(x-3)$

$2x^2 - 6x + x - 3$

$2x^2 - 5x - 3$

	$2x^2$	$-5x$	-3
x	$2x^3$	$-5x^2$	$-3x$
3	$6x^2$	$-15x$	-9

$2x^3 + 6x^2 - 5x^2 - 15x - 3x - 9$

$= 2x^3 + x^2 - 18x - 9$

(3 marks)

b) Factorise fully.

$$3x^3 - 48x$$

$3x(x^2 - 16)$

(2 marks)
(total 5 marks)

8. Points A, B & C are such that $A(0,1), B(3,0), C(3,1)$.
   i) Plot the triangle ABC.
   ii) Reflect the triangle ABC in the line $y = -x$.

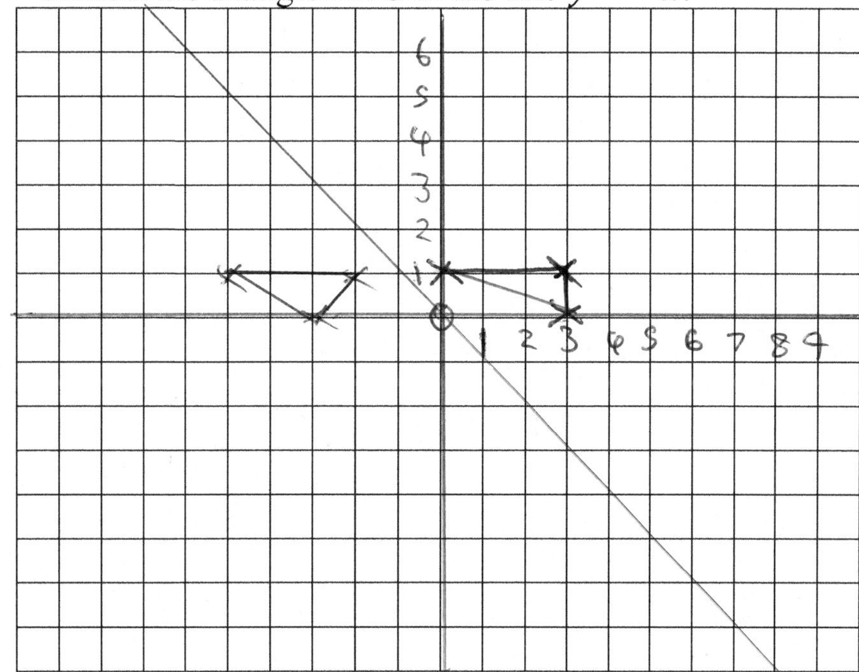

(4 marks)

9. Work out the area of the shape KLMN.

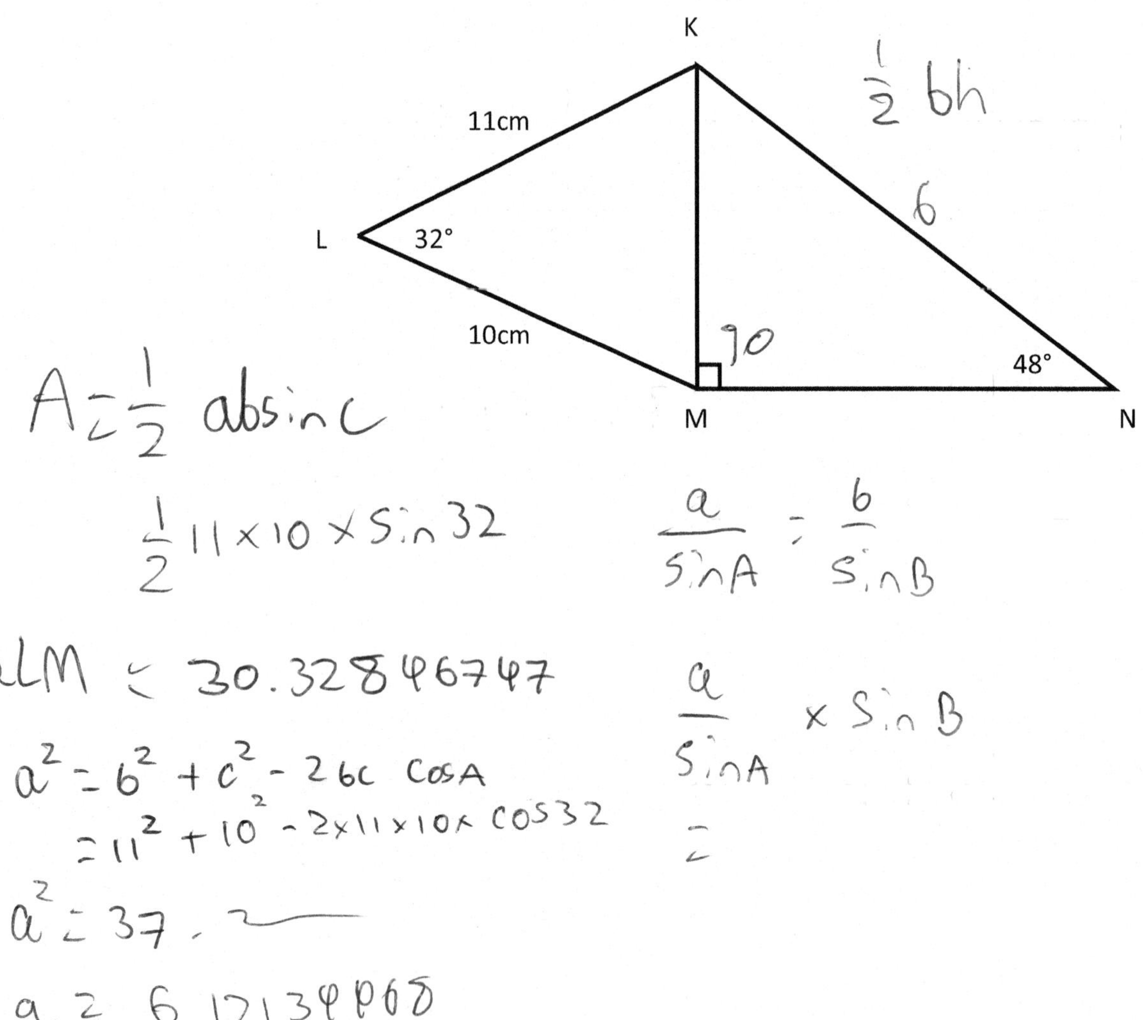

(6 marks)

10. A car is worth £18,000. It loses value by 30% every year. Max says the car will be worth less than £6,000 after 3 years. Is Max right?

(3 marks)

11. Shade the region bounded by the inequalities

$$y \leq 2x + 1, y > -x - 1 \;\&\; x < 2$$

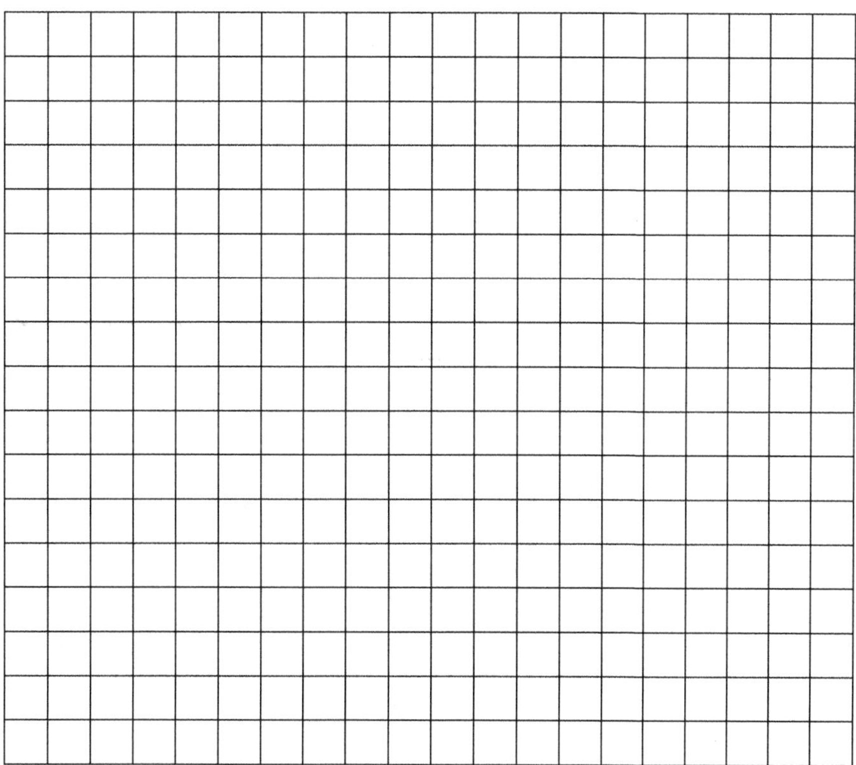

(4 marks)

12. A liquid has a density of $25g/cm^3$. Work out the volume of $10g$ of this liquid.

(3 marks)

13. Represent the following information on a histogram.

Marks	Frequency		
20-40	8		
40-70	15		
70-90	12		
90-100	6		

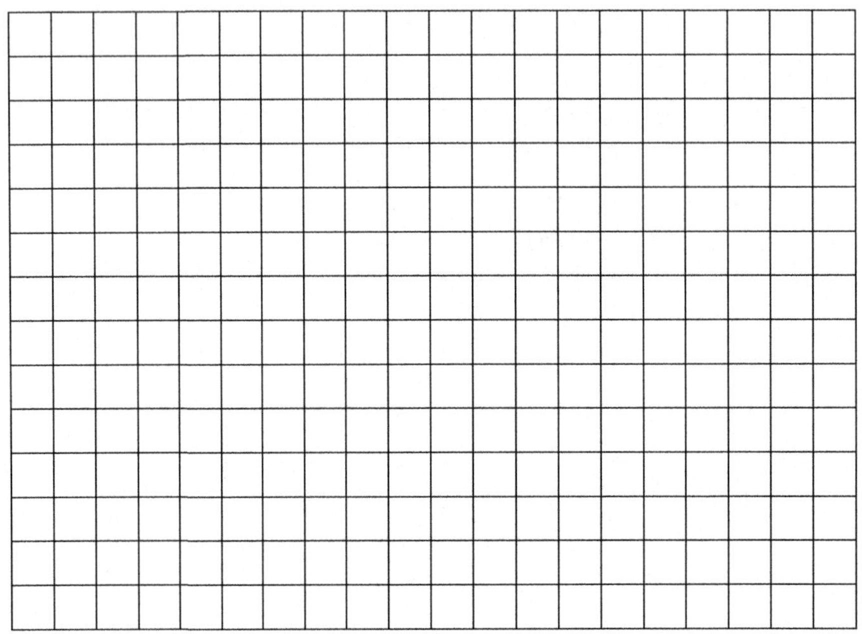

(3 marks)

14. Area of the parallelogram ABCD is $89cm^2$. Work out the value of x.

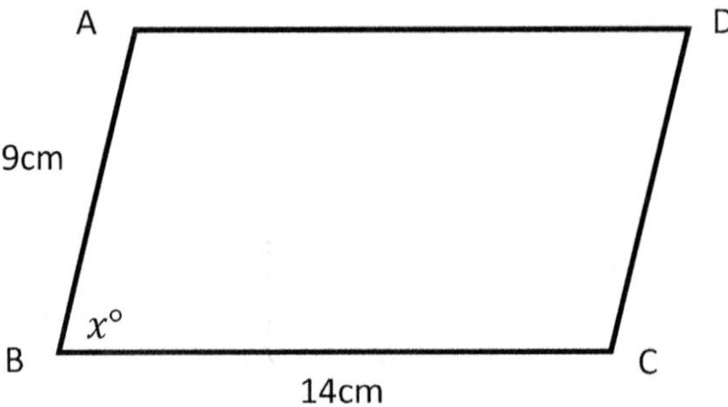

(3 marks)

15. A cylinder has radius $x\ cm$ and height $3x\ cm$.
Work out the volume of the cylinder in terms of x.

(3 marks)

16. $A = 120\ (to\ 2\ significant\ figures)$
$B = 10.4\ (to\ 1\ decemal\ place)$

Calculate the upper bound of

$$\left(\frac{AB}{A - B}\right)$$

(4 marks)

17. Work out the values of the integers a & b. Where,

$$\frac{1 + \sqrt{7}}{3 - \sqrt{7}} = a + b\sqrt{7}$$

(4 marks)

18. $y = 4x^2 - 3x + 1$

i) Find $\frac{dy}{dx}$

(2 marks)

ii) Work out the gradient, when $x = -1$.

(2 marks)

iii) Work out the x coordinate when, the gradient is zero.

(3 marks)
(total 7 marks)

19. Work out the area of the triangle ABC.

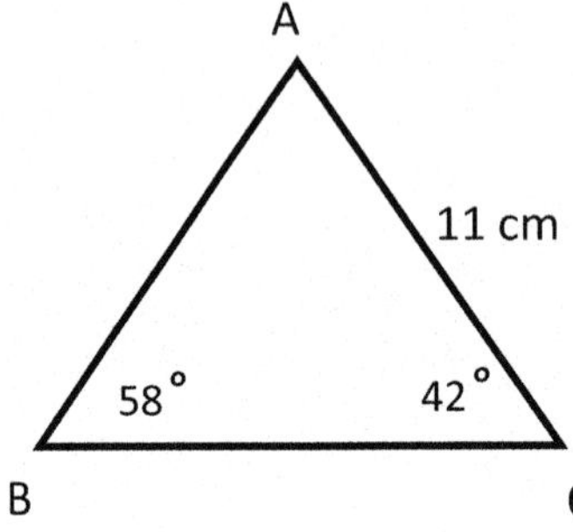

(5 marks)

20. Sketch the circle $x^2 + y^2 = 9$ and the line $y = x + 3$ on the same axes showing any points of intersections with coordinate axes.

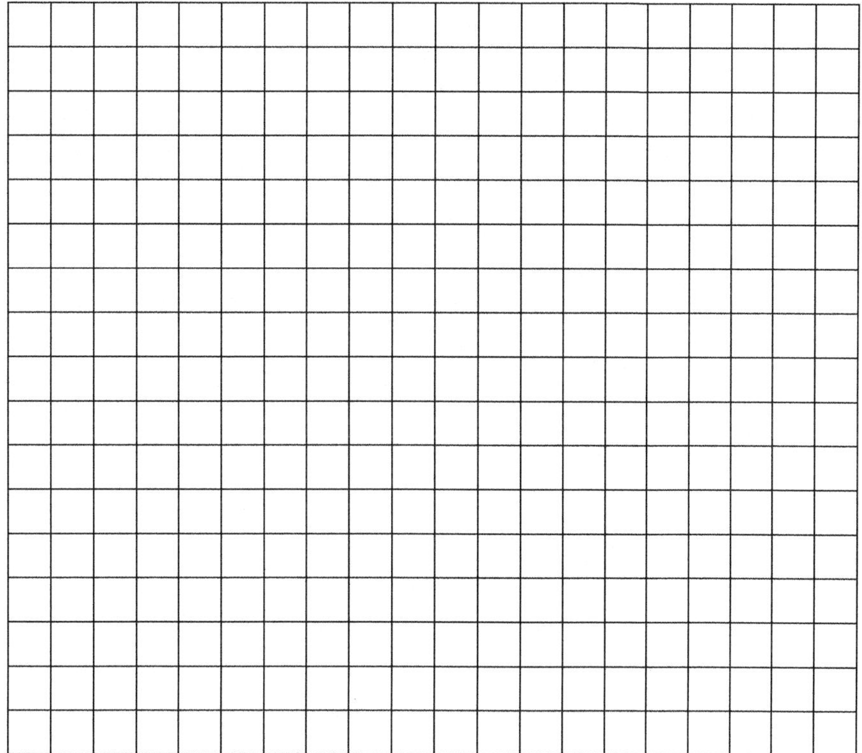

(4 marks)

21. The functions f & g are given below.

$$f(x) = \frac{x+3}{x-1}, x \neq 1 \ \& \ g(x) = 3x - 1$$

i) Work out $fg(x)$

(2 marks)

ii) Find $f^{-1}(x)$

(3 marks)
(total 5 marks)

22. On the diagram below, vectors $\overrightarrow{OA} = a$ & $\overrightarrow{OB} = b$.
C is the midpoint of OA & the ratio of $AD : DB = 3 : 1$.
Work out the Vector $\overrightarrow{CD}$.

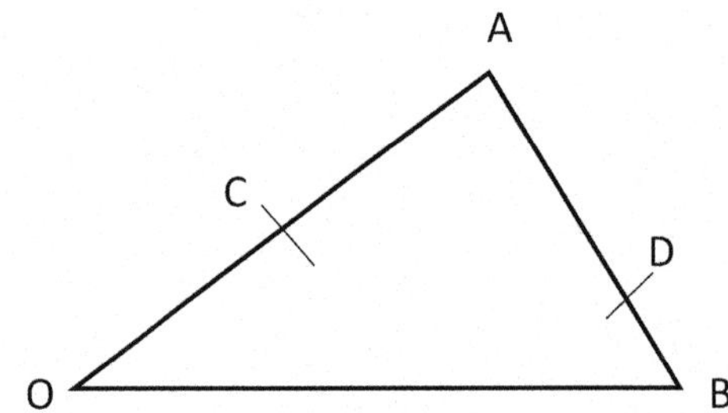

(5 marks)

23. Solve the following simultaneous equations.

$$xy = 78$$
$$y - x = 7$$

(5 marks)

Total for paper: 100 marks

End

IGCSE Mathematics
Paper 2
(calculator)

Potential Paper A2

June 2021

You must have: Ruler graduated in centimetres and millimetres, protractor, pair of compasses, pen, HB pencil, eraser.

Calculator is allowed

Time allowed
2 hours
Total 100 marks

Write answers to 3 significant figures unless stated otherwise

1. Work out the following
   i) $2a^5b^6c^7 \times 14a^{-2}b^8c^{-3}$

(3 marks)

   ii) $\left(\frac{2x^5}{3y^2}\right)^3$

(3 marks)
(total 6 marks)

2. Convert the following to m^3
   i) $2.5km^3$

(2 marks)

   ii) $4600cm^3$

(2 marks)
(total 4 marks)

3. Show that

$$3\frac{3}{4} \div \left(2\frac{1}{2} - 1\frac{2}{3}\right) = 4\frac{1}{2}$$

(4 marks)

4. Work out the value of x in each triangle.

i)

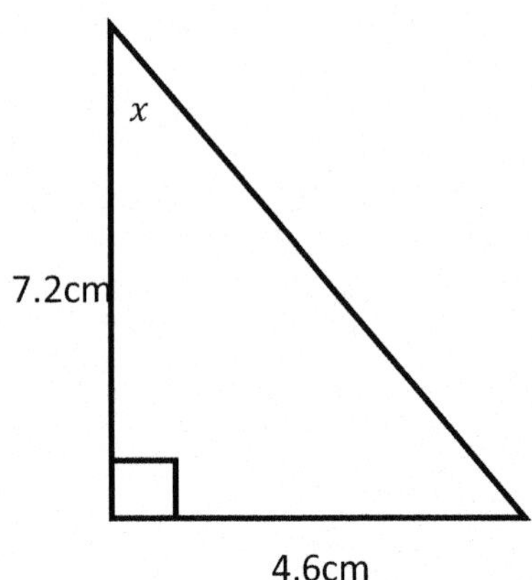

(3 marks)

ii)

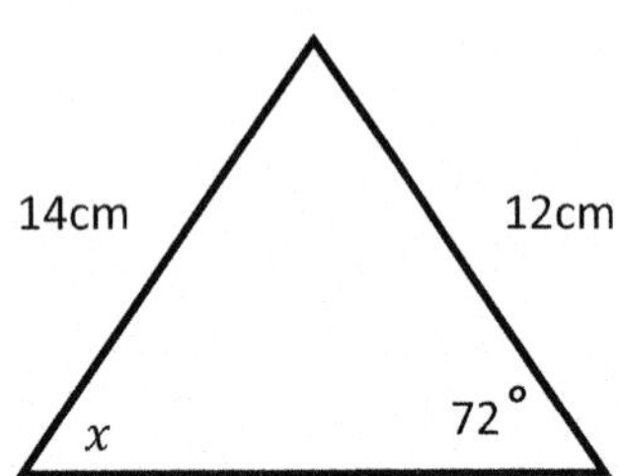

(3 marks)
(total 6 marks)

5. Construct a rectangle with length 7.8cm & width 3.4cm.

(4 marks)

6. A bag has 3 green buttons and 4 red buttons. Joseph takes a button, check its colour, and replaces it. He then takes another button.
   i) Draw a tree diagram to show all possible outcomes for the 2 buttons.

(3 marks)

   ii) What is the probability of picking at least 1 green button?

(3 marks)
(total 6 marks)

7. i) Solve the following inequality

$$x^2 - 1 > 0$$

(3 marks)

   ii) Solve the following equation by completing the square.

$$x^2 - 4x + 1 = 0$$

(4 marks)
(total 7 marks)

8. Andrew bought a bungalow for £225,000.
After 1 year, the bungalow was valued at £234,000
After 2 years, the bungalow was valued at £245,700.

Which year had the higher percentage increase?
(show your working clearly)

(3 marks)

9. Ben drove a car for 1 hour and 30 minutes and covered 96km.
i) Calculate his speed in km/h.

(2 marks)

ii) Convert your answer to part (i) to m/s.

(2 marks)
(total 4 marks)

10. A sphere has a surface area of

$$\frac{81\pi}{4}cm^2.$$

Work out the volume of the sphere?

(4 marks)

11. A laptop costs £750 in the UK and the same laptop costs €820 in France.
The exchange rate is £1 = €1.1

Which country has the better value for the laptop?

(3 marks)

12. Prove that the angle in a semi circle is always a right angle.

(4 marks)

13. Sketch the graph of $y = \sin x$ for x values between 0 & 360°.

(3 marks)

14. Dom rolled a six sided dice 2 times. Work out the probability of getting a prime number both times.

(3 marks)

15. Make (a) the subject of the formula.

$$b = \sqrt{\frac{2a^2 - 1}{5a^2 - 3}}$$

(3 marks)

16. Prove that the sum of 3 consecutive integers is always a multiple of 3.

(4 marks)

17. Following table shows information about some scores in a game.

Score	Frequency	
200-220	2	
220-300	4	
300-340	9	
340-360	7	
360-400	2	

i) Draw a cumulative frequency curve for the scores.

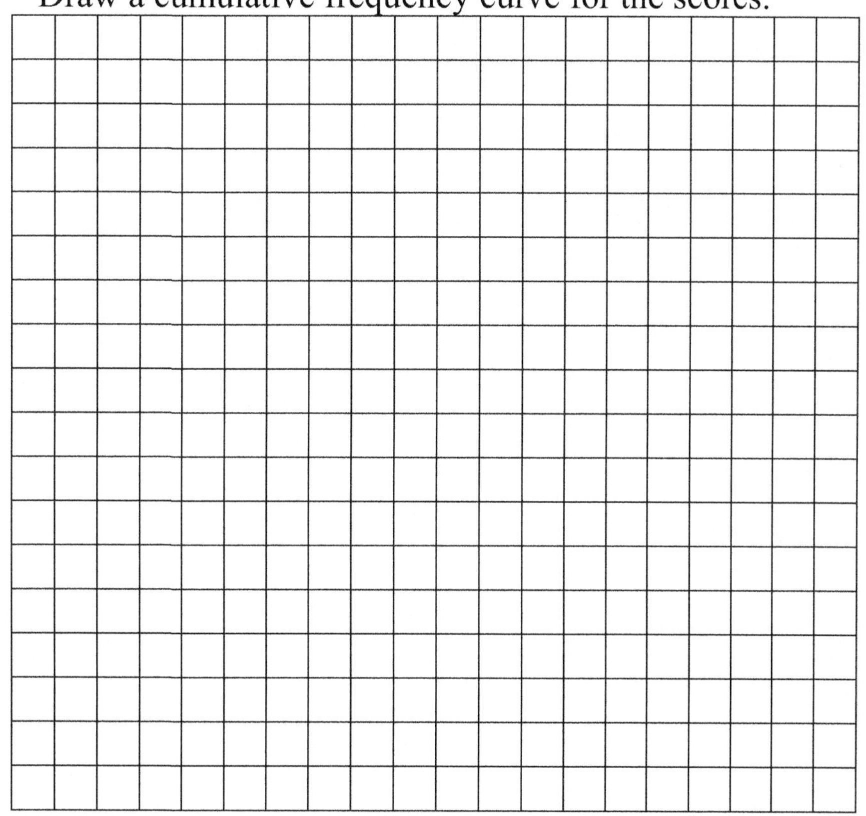

(2 marks)

ii) Find the median score

(2 marks)

iii) Find the interquartile range for the scores

(3 marks)

iv) What percentage of the scores are over 330?

(2 marks)
(total 9 marks)

18. Area of the triangle below is

$$\frac{7-\sqrt{5}}{2}cm^2$$

Find the value of x.

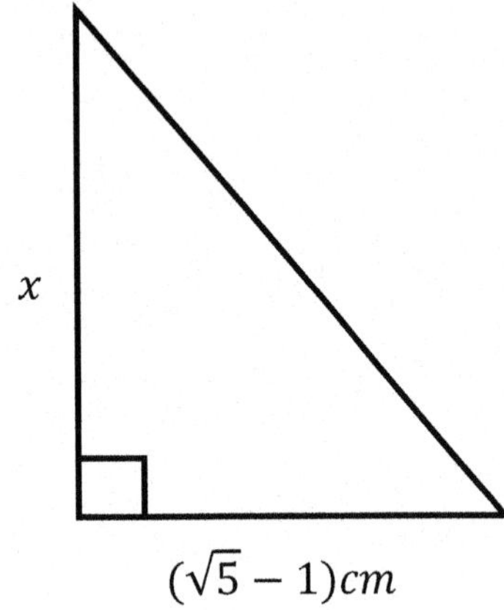

(5 marks)

19.Simplify the following fully.

$$\frac{4x^2-9}{x^2+7x+12} \div \frac{2x^2-7x-15}{x^2-16}$$

(4 marks)

20. $y = f(x)$ is sketched below.

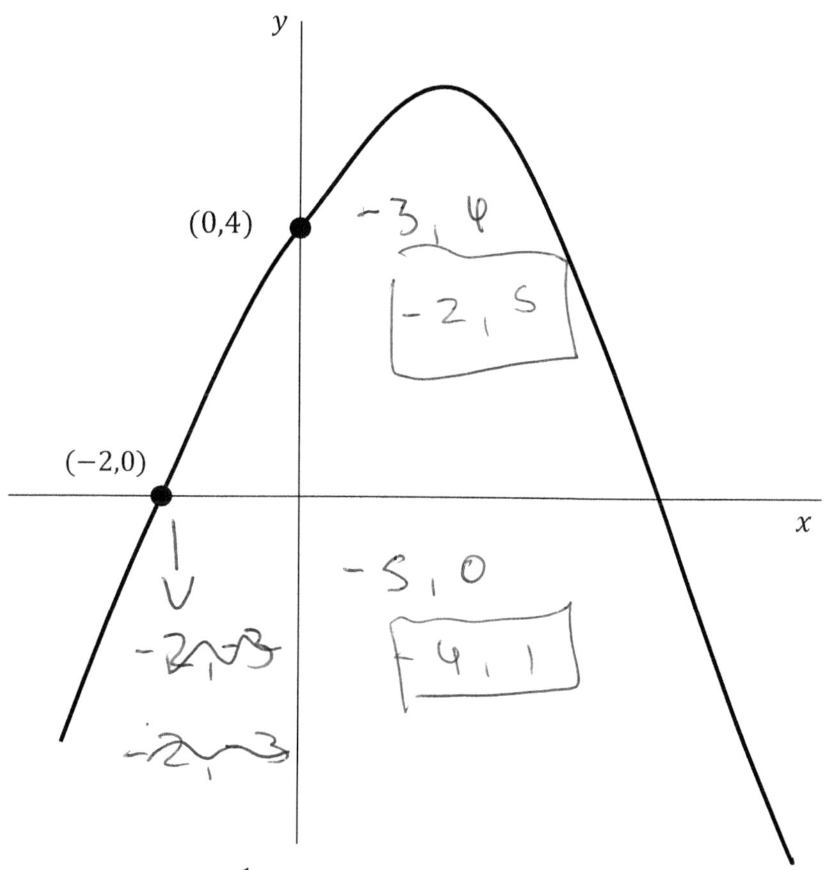

Sketch the graph of $y = \frac{1}{2}f(x-3)+1$

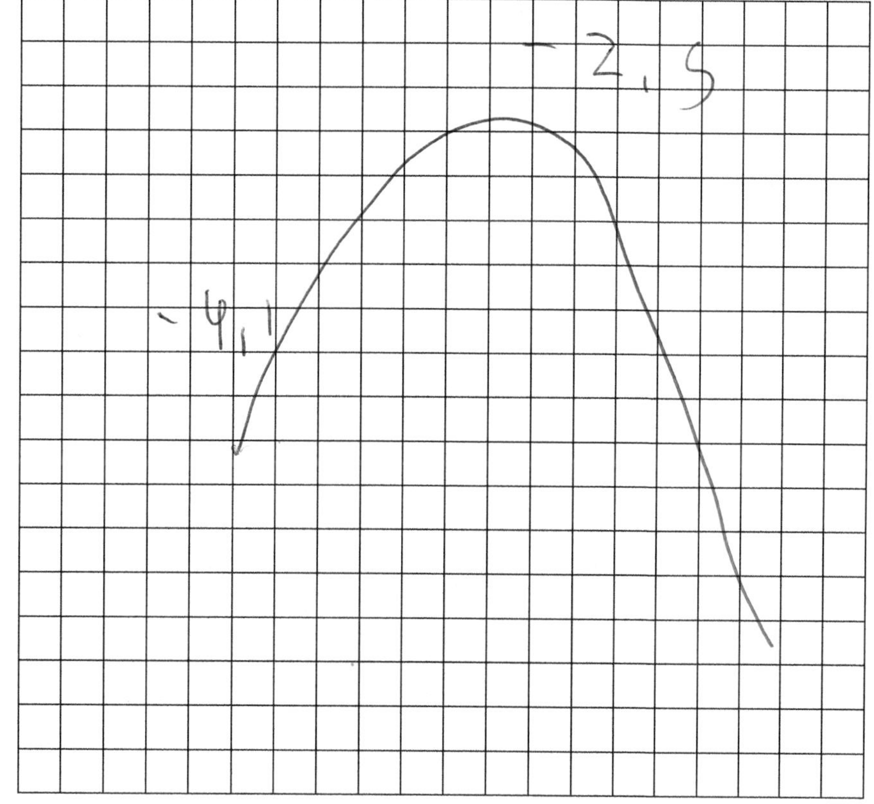

(4 marks)

21. Solve the following simultaneous equations.

i) $2x - 7y = -9$
$5x - 3y = -8$

(4 marks)

ii) $x^2 + y^2 = 53$
$y - 3x = 1$

(6 marks)
(total 10 marks)

Total for paper: 100 marks

End

Section B

IGCSE Mathematics
Paper 1
(calculator)

Potential Paper B1

June 2021

You must have: Ruler graduated in centimetres and millimetres, protractor, pair of compasses, pen, HB pencil, eraser.

Calculator is allowed

Time allowed
2 hours
Total 100 marks

Write answers to 3 significant figures unless stated otherwise

1. Solve to find x

$$\frac{2x-1}{3x+5}=\frac{3}{11}$$

(3 marks)

2. A liquid with density $4g/cm^3$ is filled into a cylinder with radius 3cm and height 8cm. Work out the mass of the liquid?

(4 marks)

3. Factorise fully

$i)\ 9x^2-25$

(2 marks)

$ii)\ 4x^2-4x-3$

(3 marks)

$iii)\ a^2+6ab+9b^2$

(3marks)

(total8 marks)

4. An interior angle of a regular polygon is 144°. Work out the number of sides of the polygon.

(3 marks)

5. Show that

$$4\frac{2}{3} \div \left(3\frac{3}{4} - 1\frac{5}{6}\right) = 2\frac{10}{23}$$

(3 marks)

6. John drove 30km/h for 10 minutes to the shop from his work. He spent 15 minutes in the shop. He then returned home 40km/h for 30 minutes. Calculate the total distance from work to his home.

(4 marks)

7. Simplify fully

i) $(3x^5y^4)^3$

(2 marks)

ii) $(3x-1)^2-(4x+3)(2x-1)$

(4 marks)

(total 6 marks)

8. i. Complete the table below for $y = x^2 - 2x - 3$

y	-2	-1	0	1	2	3	4
x							

(2 marks)

ii. On the grid below, plot the graph of $y = x^2 - 2x - 3$

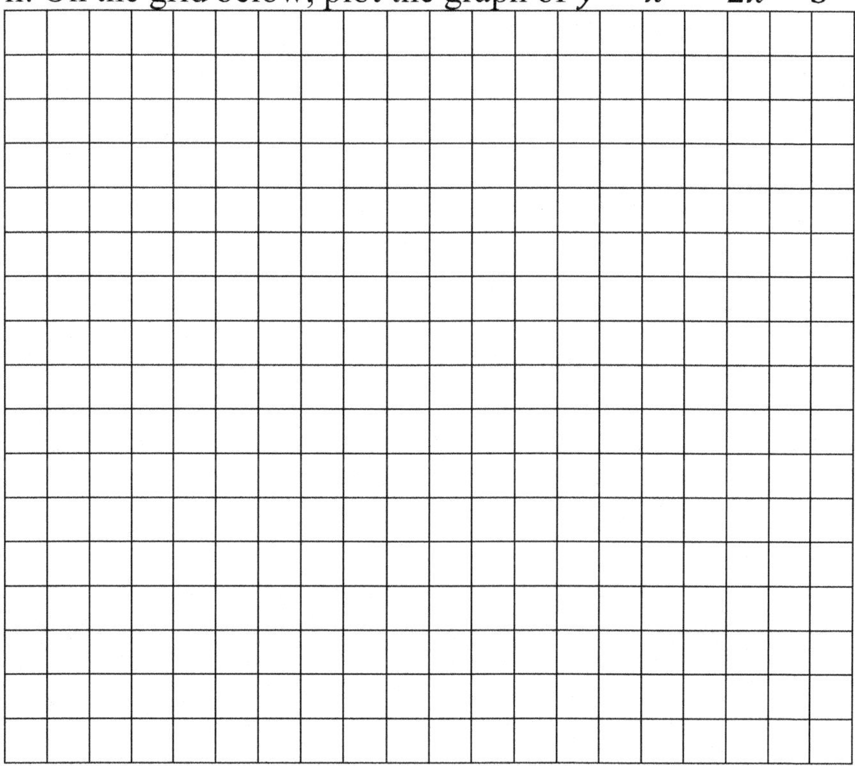

(3 marks)

(total 5 marks)

9. Andrew is likely to win 1 in 3 matches, he plays. Calculate the probability of him winning 2 consecutive matches.

(2 marks)

10. i. Write 0.00234 in standard form.

(1 mark)

ii. Write 2.34×10^4 in ordinary form.

(1 mark)

iii. Work out

$$\frac{(2.5 \times 10^5) \times (7 \times 10^{-3})}{5 \times 10^{-2}}$$

(2 marks)

(total 4 marks)

11. A bank offers 5% compound interest for first 2 years and 3.5% compound interest after that.

Jacquelyn invested £2800 for 6 years. Work out her balance after 6 years.

(4 marks)

12. Work out the area of triangle ACD.

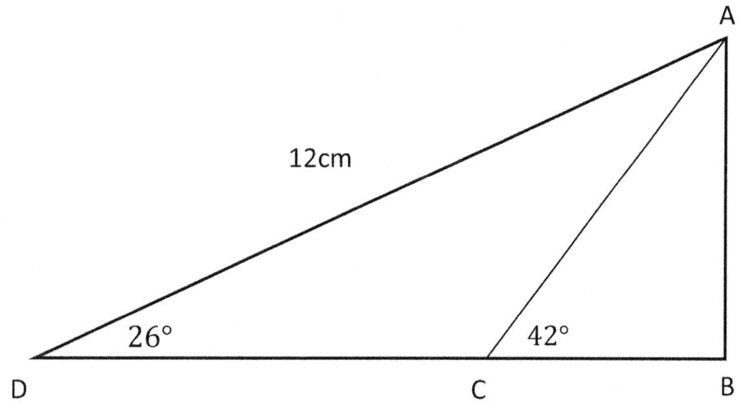

(5 marks)

13. Work out highest common factor (HCF) and lowest common multiple (LCM) of 120 and 280.

(4 marks)

14. The radius of a sphere is 4cm to nearest centimetre.
i) Work out the upper bound for the surface area of this sphere.

(2 marks)

ii) Workout the lower bound for the volume of this sphere.

(2 marks)
(total 4 marks)

15. $x^2 - 12x + 7 = (x - a)^2 + b$. Find the constants a & b.

(4 marks)

16. Show that

$$0.2\dot{5} = \frac{23}{90}$$

(2 marks)

17. ε = {integers 1 to10}, A – {even numbers}, B = {prime numbers}
a. Complete the Venn diagram

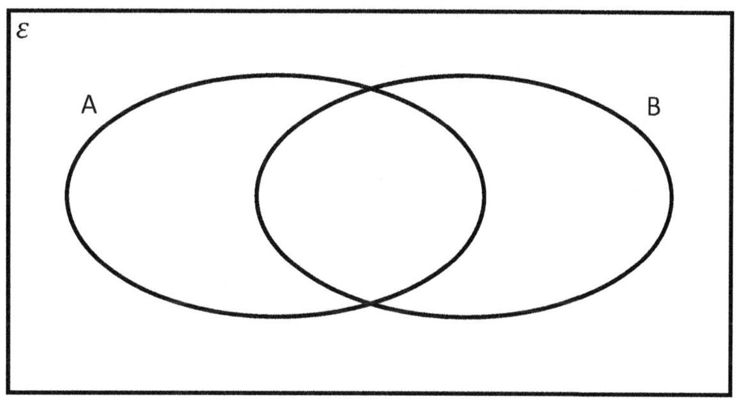

(2 marks)

b. Work out the probability of A & B.

(2 marks)
(total 4 marks)

18. Here are the first 5 terms of an arithmetic sequence.

$$8, 11, 14, 17, 20$$

Find the sum of the first 25 terms of the sequence.

(3 marks)

19. Find PQ & RT.

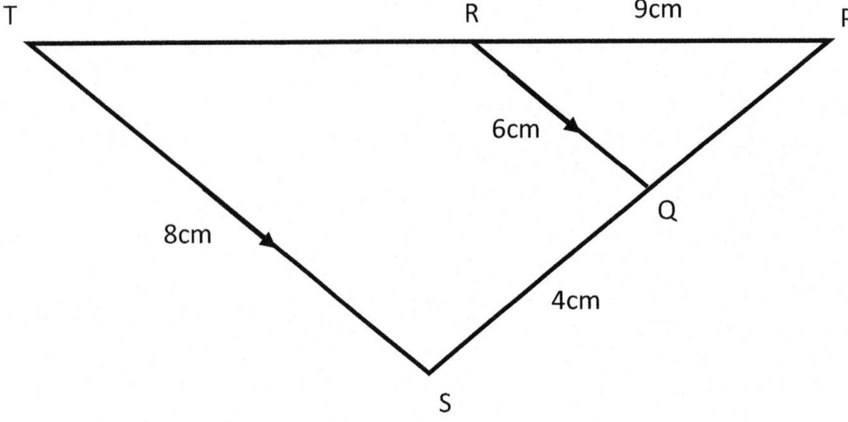

(4 marks)

20. Work out the area of triangle ABC.

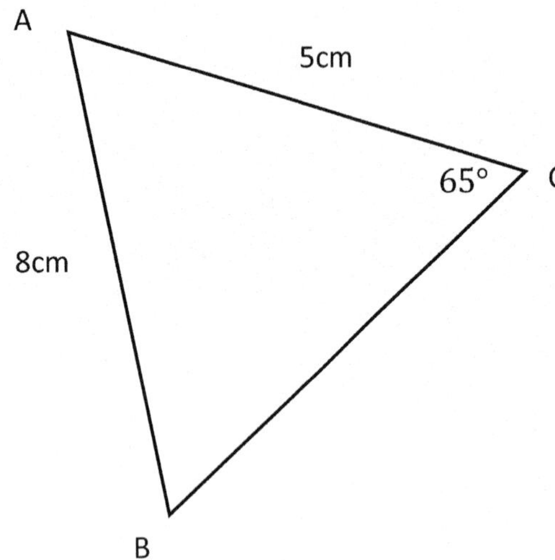

(4 marks)

21. Prove that the sum of any 2 odd numbers will always be an even number.

(3 marks)

22. Represent the following data on a histogram.

Height (cm)	Frequency	Class Width	Frequency Density
120-150	6		
150-160	7		
160-170	8		
170-190	4		
190-220	3		

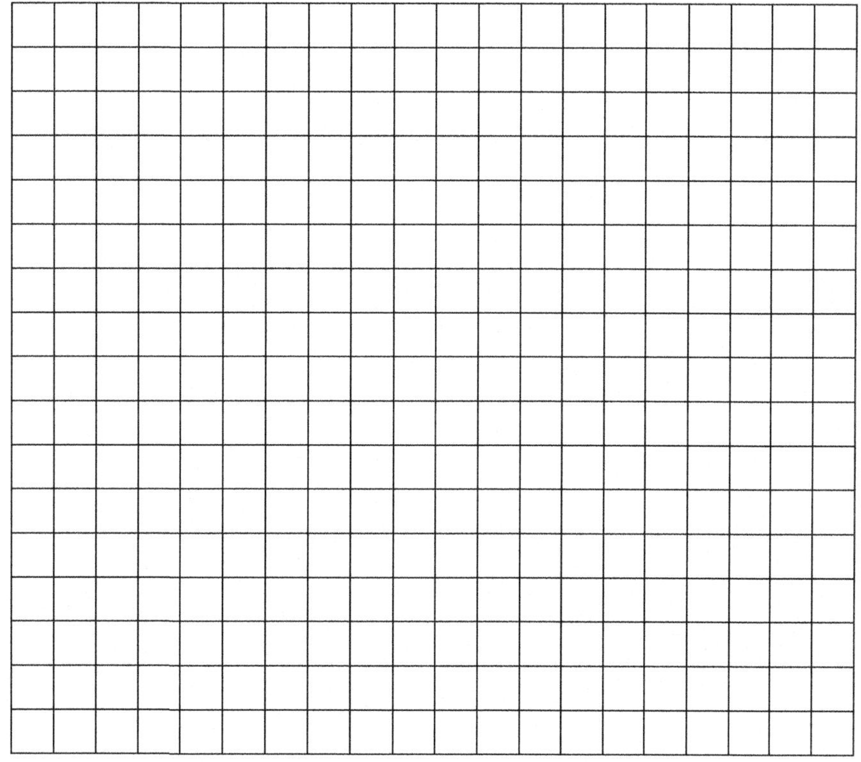

(4 marks)

23. Work out the angles CBD, ABD, ACD & BDC. Where O is the centre of the circle.
Give reasons for each stage of your calculations.

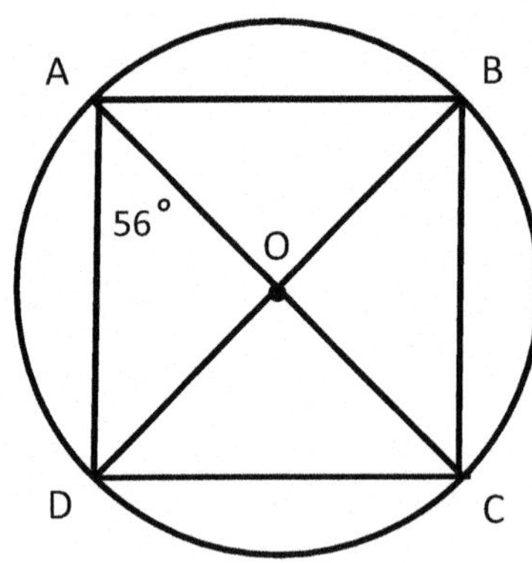

(6 marks)

24. Sketch the graph of $y = \cos x$ in the space below for x values between $0°\ to\ 360°$.

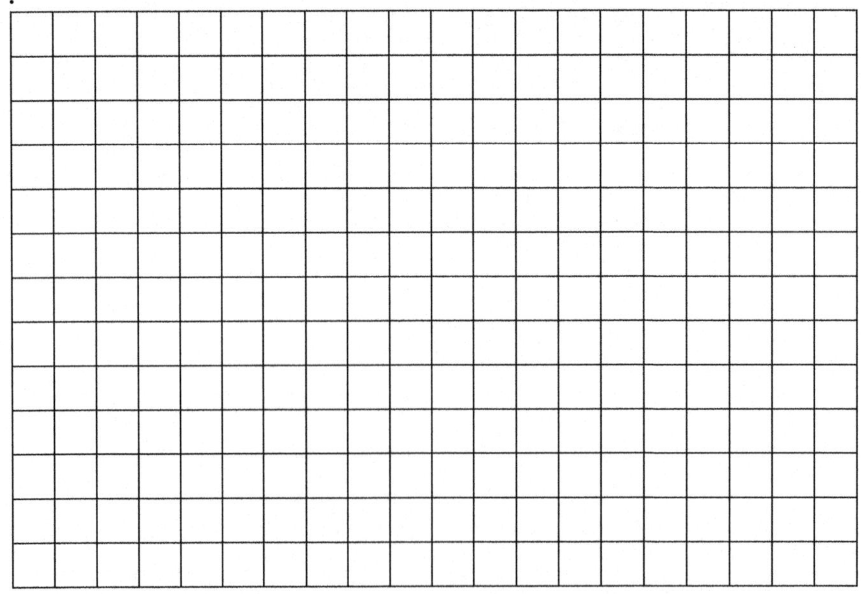

(2 marks)

25. A sphere has a radius of 6cm. the sphere is melted down and made into a cylinder with height 12cm.

i) Work out the radius of the cylinder to 2 decimal places.

(3 marks)

ii) Hence, calculate the surface area of the cylinder.

(2 marks)
(total 5 marks)

Total for paper: 100 marks

End

IGCSE Mathematics
Paper 2
(calculator)

Potential Paper B2

June 2021

You must have: Ruler graduated in centimetres and millimetres, protractor, pair of compasses, pen, HB pencil, eraser.

Calculator is allowed

Time allowed
2 hours
Total 100 marks

Write answers to 3 significant figures unless stated otherwise

1. Work out the mean salary.

Salary (£)	Frequency		
100-200	7	150	1050
200-400	12	300	3600
400-500	6	450	2700
500-800	4	650	2600
800-1000	2	900	1800
	31		20750

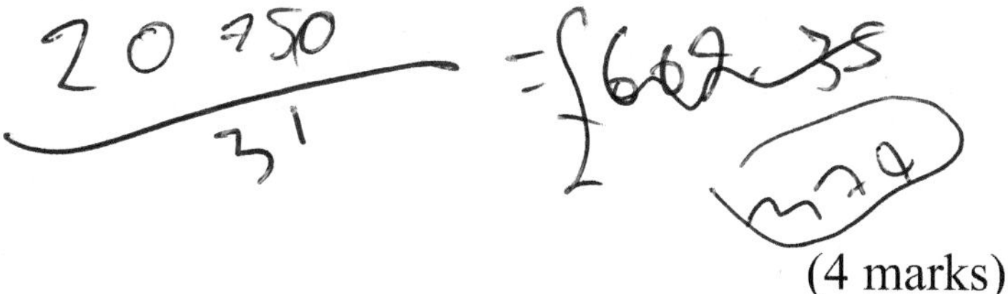

(4 marks)

2. Triangle ABC has lengths AB = 6cm, BC = 8cm & angle BAC = 60°.
Construct triangle ABC.

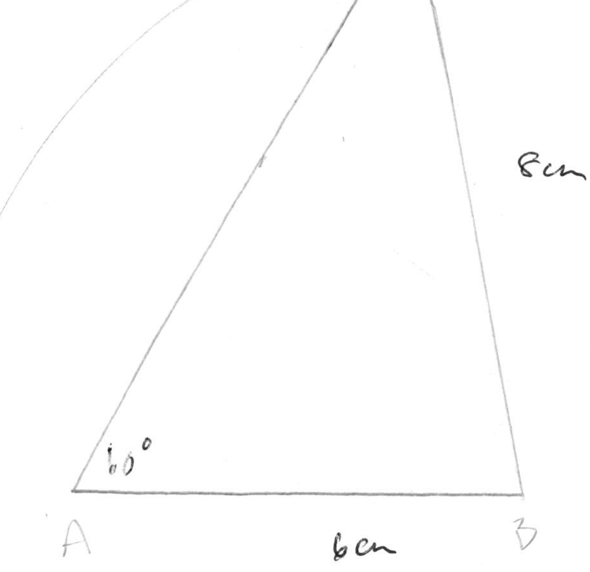

(4 marks)

3. Results from a survey of 15 people is represented in the Venn diagram below. T represents the people who has televisions and L represents the people who has laptops.

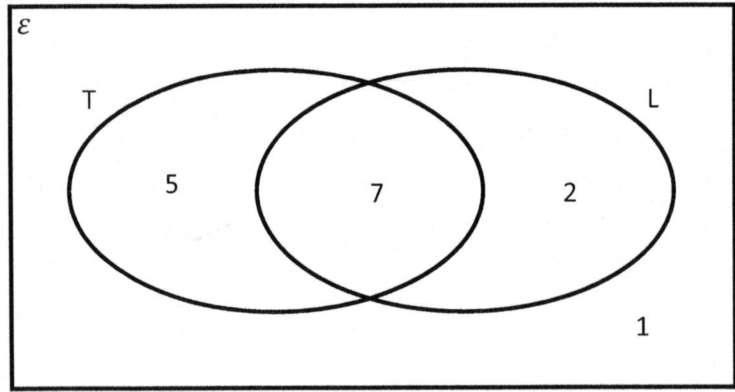

Work out the probability of someone having a television but not a laptop.

$\frac{5}{15} = \frac{1}{3}$

(2 marks)

4. A sphere has radius 4cm. It is melted down and made into a cube of length $x$cm. Find the value of x.

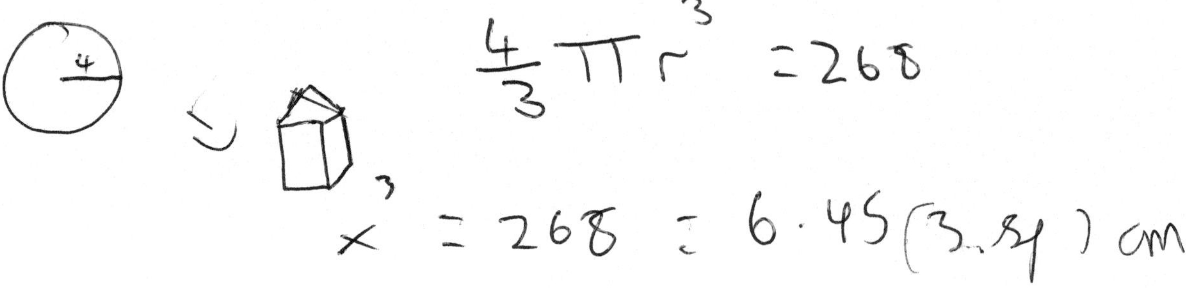

(4 marks)

5. Basil bought an apartment for £150,000 and sold it for £180,000. Work out the percentage of profit.

20%

(3 marks)

6. Area of triangle PQR is equal to the area of trapezium ABCD drawn below. Calculate the value of h.

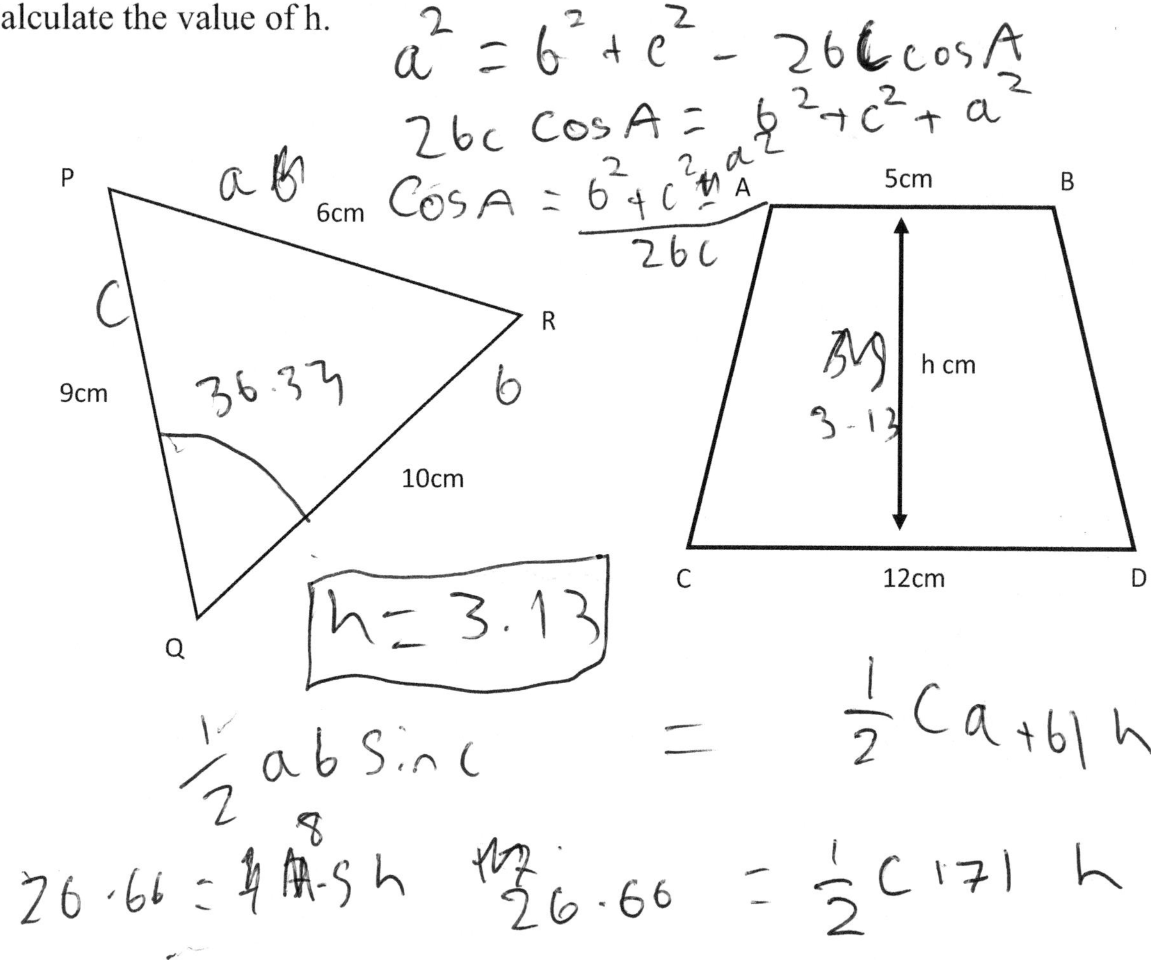

(5 marks)

7. A train travels at 120km/h. Change the speed of the train to m/s.

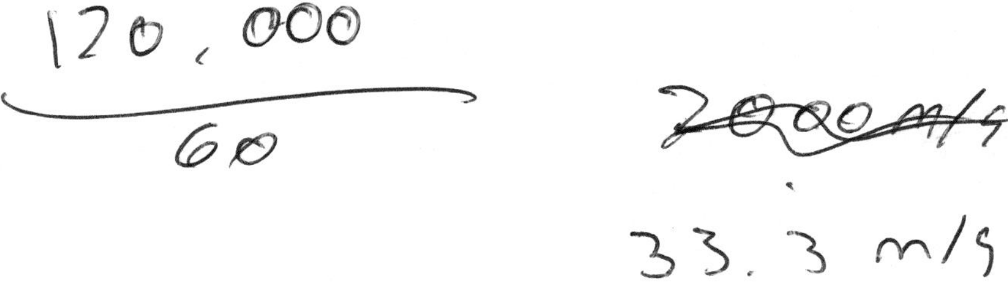

(3 marks)

8. A batsman averages 26.5 runs per innings in 8 innings. He then scored 8 in his 9th innings. After his 10th innings his average dropped to 25. Calculate the number of runs he has scored in his 10th innings?

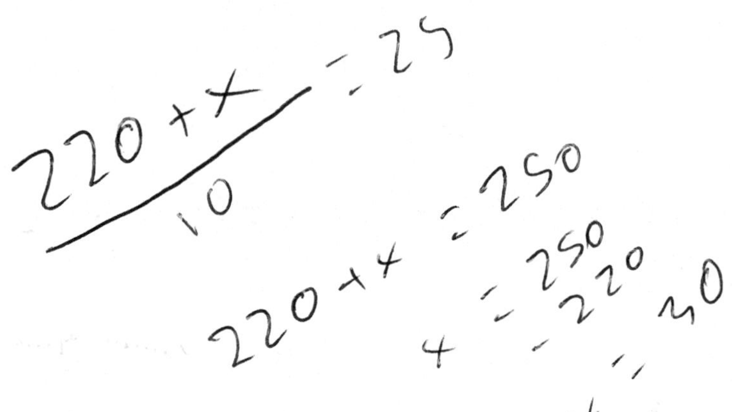

(3 marks)

9. Solve the simultaneous equation below

$$x^2 + y^2 = 61$$
$$y - x = 1$$

$y = 6$
$y = -5$
$x = -6$
$x = 5$

$x^2 + y^2 = 61$

$y = 1 + x$

$x^2 + (x+1)^2 = 61$

$x^2 + 1 + 2x + x^2 = 61$

$2x^2 + 2x + 1 = 61$

$2x^2 + 2x - 60 = 0$

$x^2 + x - 30 = 0$

$(x+6)(x-5)$

$x = -6 \quad x = 5$

(5 marks)

10. Points A & B is such that $A(-1,4)$ & $B(3,2)$
i) Work out the midpoint of AB

(1, 3)

(1 mark)

ii) Work out the gradient of AB

$\frac{-2}{4}$ $\left(-\frac{1}{2}\right)$

(1 mark)

iii) Find equation of perpendicular line to AB through the point $(0, 3)$

$y = mx + c$

$y = 2x + c$

$3 = 0 + c$

$y = 2x + 3$

(3 marks)
(total 5 marks)

11. A computer is £680 after a 20% discount. Work out the original price of the computer before the discount.

£850

(3 marks)

12. Work out the perimeter of the sector AOB to 3 significant figures.

$C = 2\pi r$

$\frac{38}{360} \times 2 \times \pi \times 10$

$+ 20$

26.6

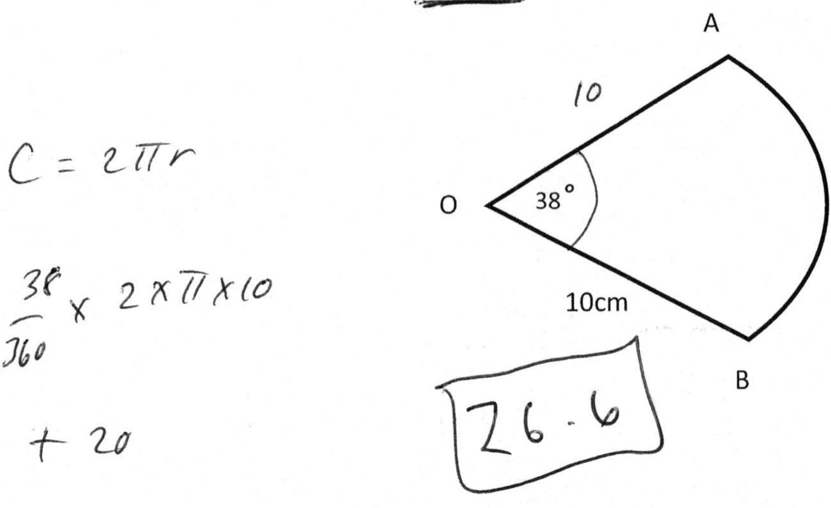

(3 marks)

13. Vector $\overrightarrow{OA} = a$ & $\overrightarrow{OB} = b$. D is the midpoint of OA & $AC:CB = 2:1$.
Work out vector $\overrightarrow{DC}$.

2 : 1 $-b + a$

$-\frac{1}{2}a + b + \frac{-b+a}{3}$

$-\frac{a}{2} + b + \frac{-b}{3} + \frac{a}{3}$

$\frac{1}{6}a + \frac{2}{3}b$

$-\frac{a}{6} + \frac{2}{3}b$

$\frac{2}{3}b - \frac{a}{6}$

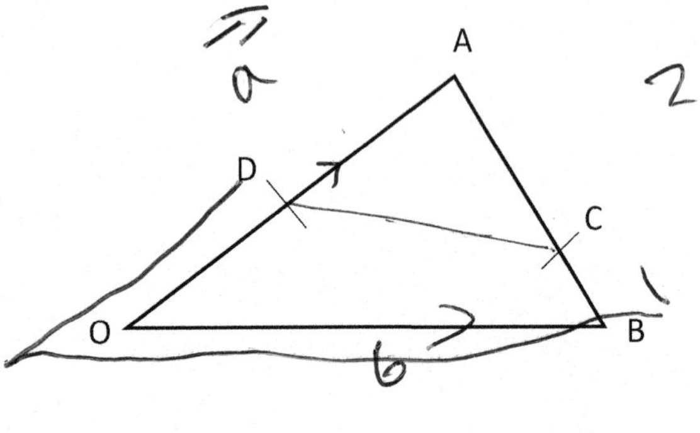

(4 marks)

14. Data for some weights are given in the table below.

Weights (g)	Frequency	
20-40	3	
40-50	6	
50-80	8	
80-90	5	
90-120	2	

i. Draw a cumulative frequency curve for above data.

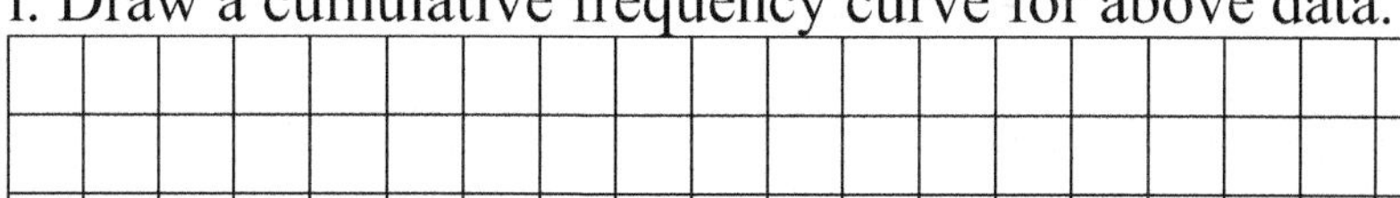

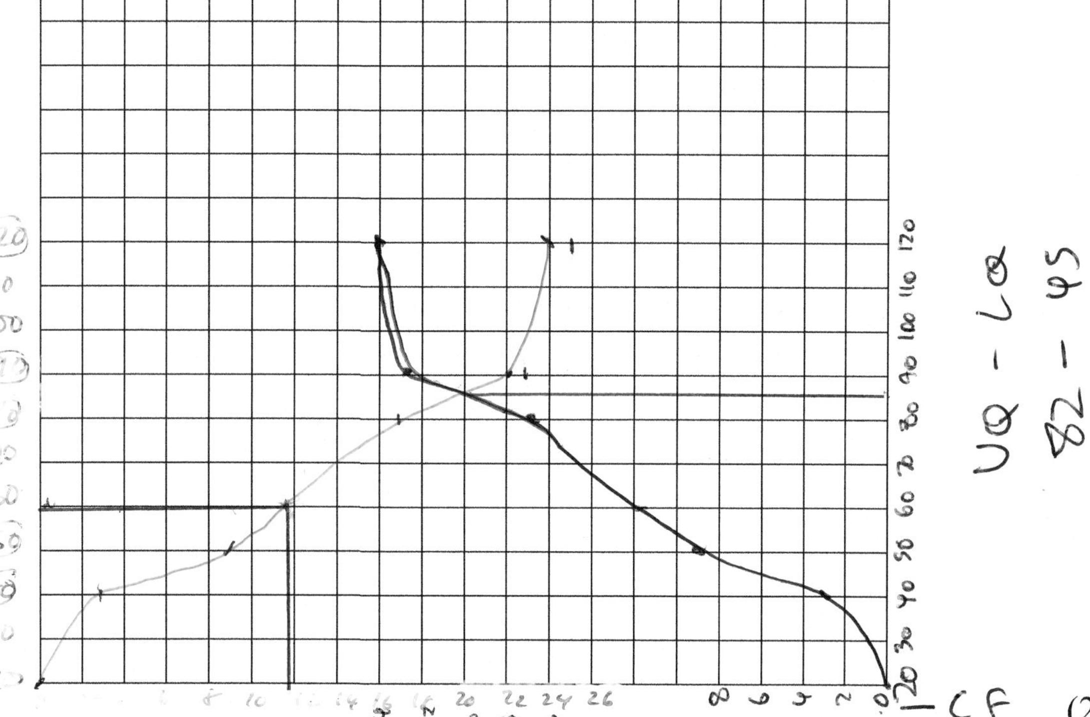

(2 marks)

ii. Work out the median weight.

(1 mark)

iii. Work out an estimate for interquartile range.

(3 marks)

iv. Calculate the percentage of weights over 85g.

(2 marks)

(total 8 marks)

15. i. Make x the subject of the formula

$$y = \sqrt{\frac{3x - 5}{x - 2}}$$

(4 marks)

ii. Hence or otherwise, calculate the value of x when $y = 2$.

(2 marks)
(total 6 marks)

16.

$$\frac{2 - \sqrt{27}}{2 + \sqrt{3}} = p + q\sqrt{3}$$

Where p & q are integers. Work out the values of p & q.

(4 marks)

17. A is inversely proportional to B^2. When $A = 6, B = 10$.
Find the values of B, when $A = 24$.

(4 marks)

18. $y = x^3 - 4x^2 + 5x - 1$
Find the value of $\frac{dy}{dx}$, when $x = 2$.

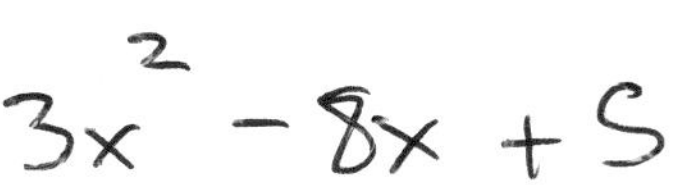

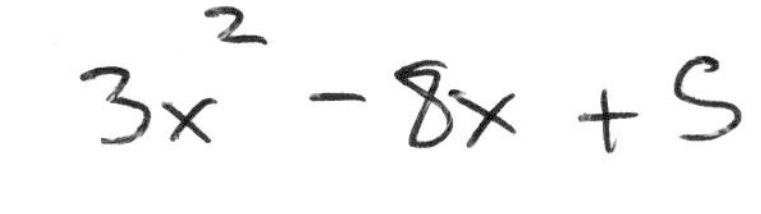

(4 marks)

19. Work out the area of quadrilateral ABCD.

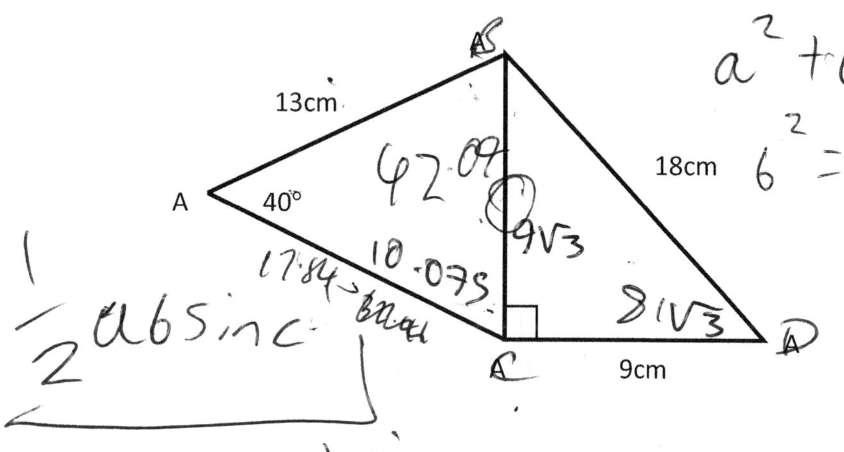

(8 marks)

20. Solve the following inequalities.
i. $x - 5 > 4 - 3x$

(2 marks)

ii. $2x^2 - 3x - 2 < 0$

(4 marks)
(total 6 marks)

21. $f(x) = x^2 - 1,\ g(x) = 2x + 5$
Work out the following
i) $gf(x)$

(2 marks)

ii) $g^{-1}(x)$

(2 marks)

iii) $fg(2)$

(2 marks)
(total 6 marks)

22. A cone has radius 3cm & vertical height 12cm and a cylinder has height 6cm. Given that the volume of the cone is exactly the same as the volume of the cylinder.

i. Calculate the radius of the cylinder.

(4 marks)

ii. Hence, work out the surface area of the cylinder.

(2marks)
(total 6 marks)

Total for paper: 100 marks

End

Section C

IGCSE Mathematics
Paper 1
(calculator)

Potential Paper C1

May 2021

You must have: Ruler graduated in centimetres and millimetres, protractor, pair of compasses, pen, HB pencil, eraser.

Calculator is allowed

Time allowed
2 hours
Total 100 marks

Write answers to 3 significant figures unless stated otherwise

1. Factorise following expressions fully

(i) $6x^3 - 9x^2$

$3x^2(2x-3)$

(1 mark)

(ii) $25y^2 - 16x^2$

$x^2y^2(25-16)$

(2 marks)

(iii) $x^2 - 3x + 2$

$(x-1)(x-2)$

(2 marks)

(iv) $5x^2 + 13x - 6$

$\times$ -30
$+$ 13

$5x^2+10x-3x-6$

-10 -3

(3 marks)
(total 8 marks)

2. Work out highest common factor and lowest common multiple for following

(i) 42 and 70

(3 marks)

(ii) 96 and 144

(4 marks)

(Total 7 marks)

3. Two functions f & g are as follows

$$f(x) = 3x - 5$$
$$g(x) = x^2$$

(i) Find $fg(x)$

$3x^2 - 5$

(2 marks)

(ii) Work out $gf(-1)$

$f(-1) = -8$

$-8^2 = 64$

$gf(-1) = 64$

(2 marks)

(iii) Find $f^{-1}(x)$

$\frac{y+5}{3} = 3x$

$f^{-1}(x) = \frac{x+5}{3}$

(2 marks)

(total 6 marks)

4. A computer is for sale after a 20% discount at £456. Calculate the original price of the computer before discount.

(3 marks)

5. A circle has an area of $176.71cm^2$.
   (i) Work out the circumference of the above circle

(3 marks)

   (ii) A rectangle has width 5.5cm and its perimeter is equal to the circumference of circle in part (i). Calculate the length of rectangle.

(3 marks)

(total 6 marks)

6. Calculate AD & AC (to 3 significant figures)

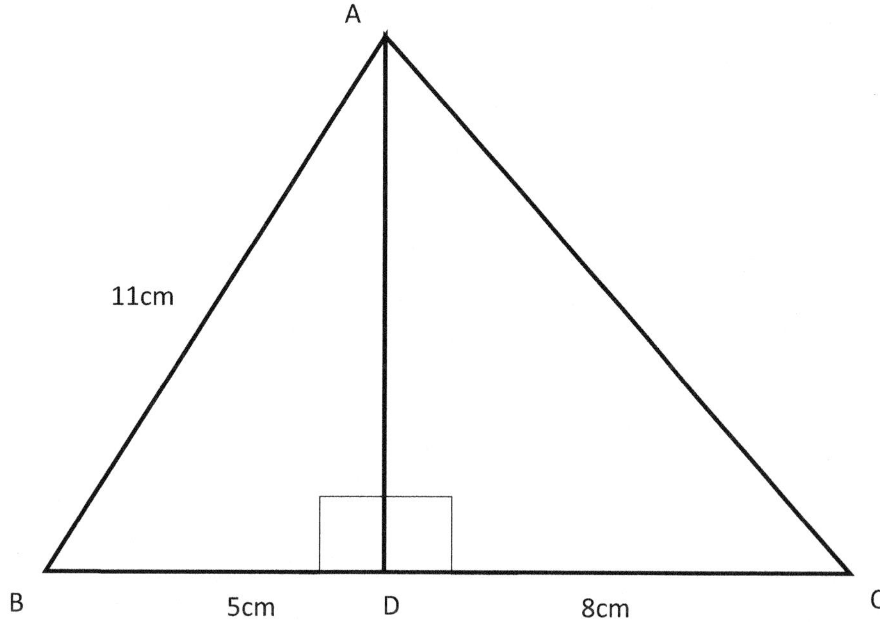

(5 marks)

7. a) write the following in standard form

(i) 2037

(ii) 23.07

(iii) 0.0237

(3 marks)

b) Write the following in ordinary form

(i) 2.037×10^{-3}

(ii) 2.307×10^{2}

(iii) $(1.45 \times 10^{4}) \div (2.9 \times 10^{-2})$

(4 marks)

(total 7 marks)

8. Make y the subject of the formula.

$$x = \frac{\sqrt{2 - 3y}}{5a}$$

(3 marks)

9. Work out

$$3\frac{1}{3} \div (2\frac{3}{4} - 1\frac{5}{6})$$

(4 marks)

10. Work out the volume of a sphere, whose surface area is same as the surface area of a solid cylinder with radius 3cm & height 8cm.

(6 marks)

11.OAB is a sector of a circle centred O.

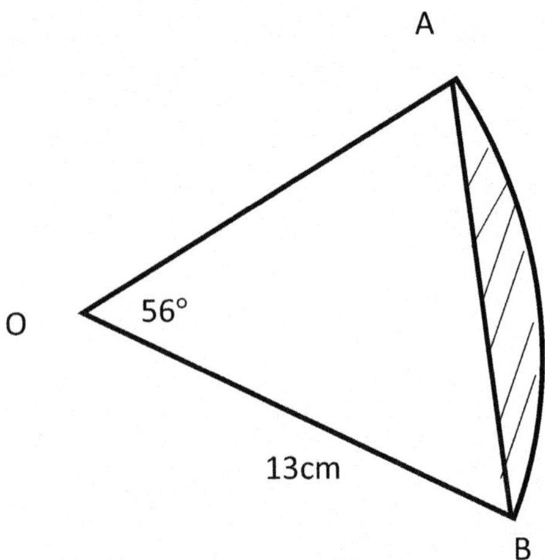

(i) Calculate the arc length AB.

(2 marks)

(ii) Calculate the length AB

(2 marks)

(iii) Calculate the area of shaded region?

(4 marks)

(total marks 8 marks)

12. The following table shows information for a company's salary structure.

Salary (£)	**Frequency**	**Cumulative Frequency**
1000-1500	2	
1500-2000	4	
2000-2500	5	
2500-3500	3	
3500-5000	1	

(i) Draw a cumulative frequency curve.

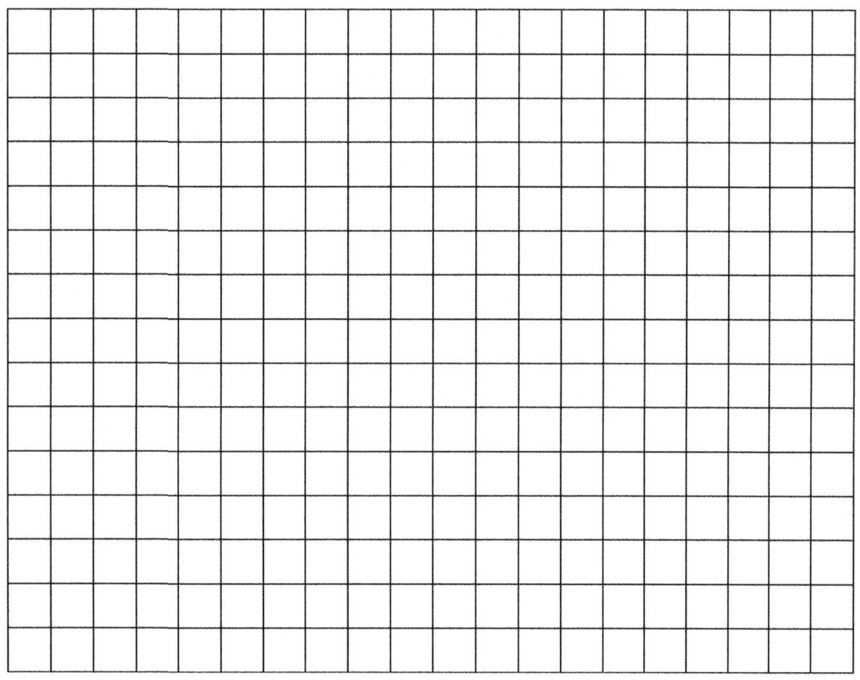

(2 marks)

(ii) Work out the median salary.

(2 marks)

(iii) Calculate the interquartile range.

(3 marks)

(total 7 marks)

13. Expand and simplify

(i) $(x+3)(x-4)-7(3x-2)$

(3 marks)

(ii) $(2x-3)^2-(x+3)(x-2)$

(4 marks)

(total 7 marks)

14. Andrew drove 80km/h for 45 minutes and then he walked 5km in 15 minutes. Calculate his average speed for the overall journey.

(4 marks)

15. Liquid P has a density of $5g/cm^3$ & liquid Q has a density of $7\ g/cm^3$.
100ml of P & 75ml of Q is mixed to make liquid R.
Work out the density of liquid R.

(5 marks)

16. Solve the following inequality and represent it on a number line.

$$-5 \leq 3x - 2 < 13$$

(4 marks)

17. A is inversely proportional to B^2 & when A = 8, B = $\frac{1}{2}$.

(i) Work out A when B = 4.

(3 marks)

(ii) Work out B when A =10.

(2 marks)

(total 5 marks)

18.Solve the following

$$xy = 15$$
$$y + 3x = 14$$

(5 marks)

Total for paper: 100 marks

End

IGCSE Mathematics
Paper 2
(calculator)

Potential Paper C2

June 2021

You must have: Ruler graduated in centimetres and millimetres, protractor, pair of compasses, pen, HB pencil, eraser.

Calculator is allowed

Time allowed
2 hours
Total 100 marks

Write answers to 3 significant figures unless stated otherwise

1. Find highest common factor and lowest common multiple of 72 & 96.

(4 marks)

2. A sequence has terms 27, 23, 19, 15, ...
   i) Find an expression for n^{th} term

(2 marks)

   ii) Is 5 a term in the sequence?

(1 mark)

(total 3 marks)

3. A cylinder has a volume of $90\pi cm^3$. The height of the cylinder is 10cm. Work out its radius?

(3 marks)

4. Solve the following equation

$$3(2x-1)+4(3x-5)=5(2x+7)$$

(4 marks)

5. A computer is £584 after a 27% discount. Calculate its original price?

(3 marks)

6. Work out the area of triangle ABC to 3 significant figures.

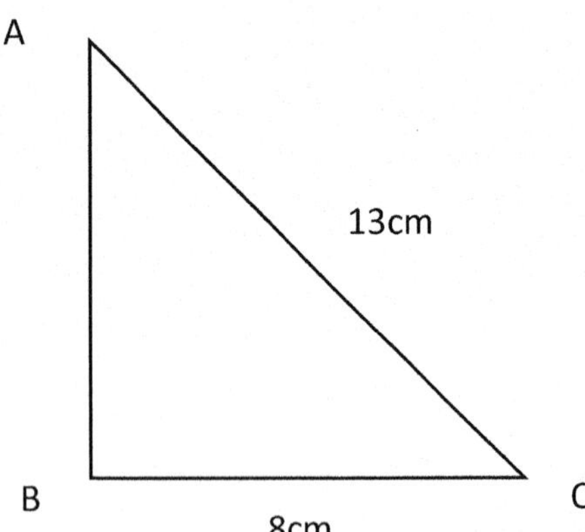

(4 marks)

7. $a = 2, b = -3, c = 5$
   Work out
   i) $a^2 - 3c$

(2 marks)

   ii) $c^2 - 2b$

(2 marks)

(total 4 marks)

8. Work out

$$\frac{(2.3 \times 10^8) \times (1.9 \times 10^{-3})}{2.5 \times 10^5}$$

(3 marks)

9. Factorise fully
   i) $9y^2 - 49$

(2 marks)

   ii) $x^2 - 2x - 195$

(2 marks)

   iii) $3x^2 - 17x + 20$

(3 marks)
(total 7 marks)

10. Write the following as fractions

i) 35%

(1 mark)

ii) 0.28

(2 marks)

iii) $0.2\dot{8}$

(3 marks)

(total 6 marks)

11. Sector OAB is shown below. Length AB is 8cm and angle AOB is 26°.

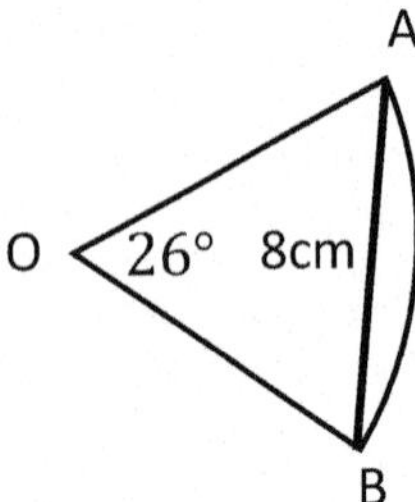

i) Work out radius of sector OAB

(3 marks)

ii) Hence or otherwise, calculate the area of sector OAB

(2 marks)

(total 5 marks)

12.Calculate area of triangle PQR.

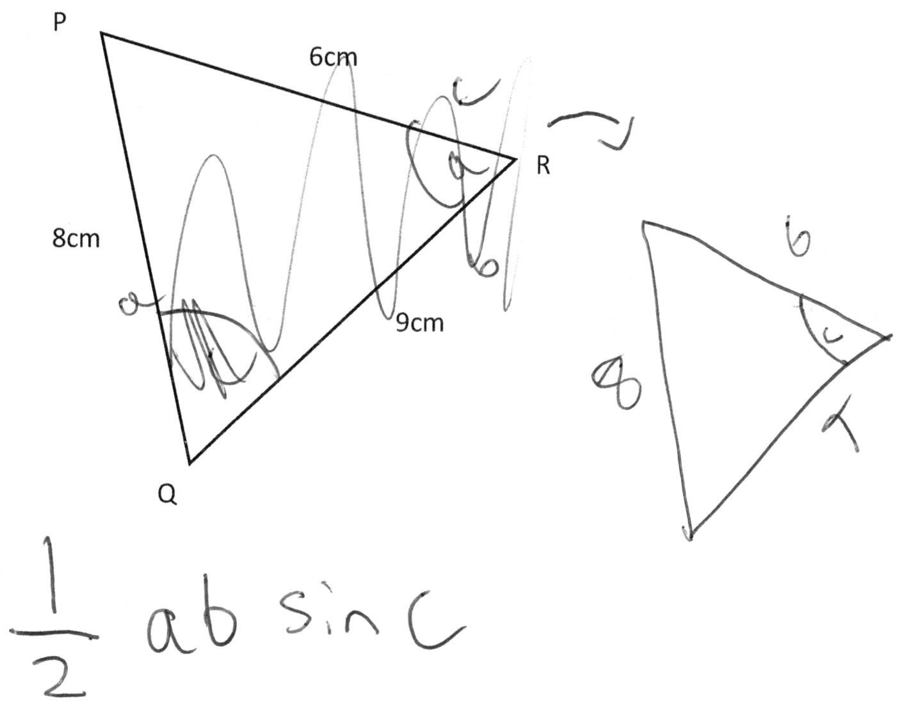

(4 marks)

13.Simplify the following

i) $(3a^2b^{-3})^3$

(2 marks)

ii) $(2x-1)^2-(x-3)(x+1)$

(3 marks)

(total 5 marks)

14. $a = \sqrt{2x^2 - b}$, make x the subject of the formula.

(3 marks)

15. Solve the following inequalities

i) $5(3x - 1) - 1 \leq 4$

(2 marks)

ii) $x^2 - 10x + 24 > 0$

(4 marks)
(total 6 marks)

16. A(3, 5), B(7, 11)

i) Find midpoint of AB

(2 marks)

ii) Work out the equation of the line AB

(4 marks)

(total 6 marks)

17. Jackie has 7 sweets in a bag. 4 of them are red and the rest are blue. She ate two sweets at random.

i) Draw a tree diagram to show all possibilities

(2 marks)

ii) Work out probability of eating one of each

(3 marks)

iii) Work out probability of eating at least one red sweet

(3 marks)

(total 8 marks)

18. $y = x^2 - 5x + 3$

i) Find $\frac{dy}{dx}$

(2 marks)

ii) Work out equation of tangent to $y \ at \ x = 3$

(4 marks)

(total 6 marks)

19. Solve the following equations

i) $2x - 3y = 0$
$5x - 2y = 11$

(3 marks)

ii) $xy = 21$
$y - x = 4$

(5 marks)
(total 8 marks)

20. a.) Simplify the following

i) $(\sqrt{2} - 1)(3 + \sqrt{2})$

(2 marks)

ii) $\sqrt{75} + \sqrt{48} - \sqrt{27}$

(2 marks)

b.) Rationalise

i) $\frac{12}{\sqrt{2}}$

(2 marks)

ii) $\frac{15-\sqrt{3}}{\sqrt{3}}$

(2 marks)

(total 8 marks)

Total for paper: 100 marks

End

Section D

IGCSE Mathematics
Paper 1
(calculator)

Potential Paper D1

May 2021

You must have: Ruler graduated in centimetres and millimetres, protractor, pair of compasses, pen, HB pencil, eraser.

Calculator is allowed

Time allowed
2 hours
Total 100 marks

Write answers to 3 significant figures unless stated otherwise

1. Arithmetic sequence has 4th term 17 and 7th term 29.

   (i) Work out the first term and the common difference.

   29
   17
   12 / 3 = 4

   First term = 5
   Common difference = 4

   5, 9, 13, 17 = 4n + 1

   (4 marks)

   (ii) Work out the sum of the first 10 terms.

   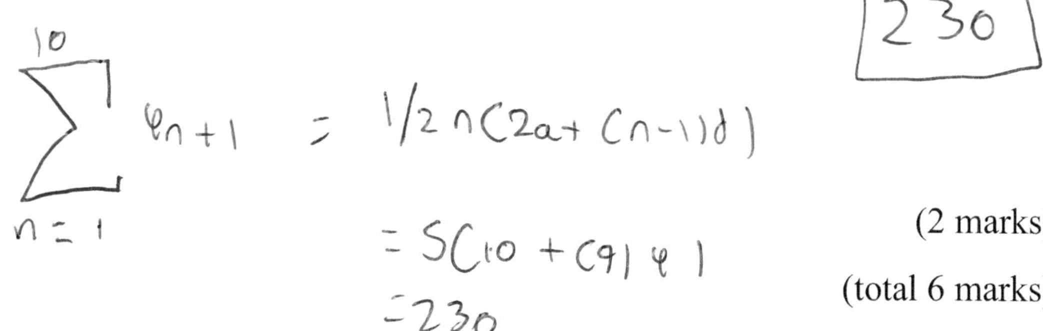

   $\sum_{n=1}^{10} 4n+1 = \frac{1}{2}n(2a+(n-1)d)$

   $= 5(10 + (9)4)$

   $= 230$

   230

   (2 marks)

   (total 6 marks)

2. A, B & C shared £x in ratio 3:5:6. B received £30 more than A. Work out x?

   X = 15

   A : B : C

   3x : 5x : 6x

   2x = 30
   x = 15

   (3 marks)

3. Jenny bought 1kg of flour for £2.39, 1 tub of butter for £3.39 & 500g of sugar for £1.45 to bake a cake. She cut 40 slices from the cake and sold 30 of them for £1.25 each and the rest for 75p each. Calculate her total profit.

   Spent
   1kg f = £2.39
   1 tub = £3.39
   500g s = £1.45
   £7.23

   Sold
   30 × 1.25 = 37.5
   10 × 0.75 = 7.50
   45

   Profit = Sold − spent
   = £37.77

   (4 marks)

4. Calculate PS & PR

$\frac{a}{\sin A} = \frac{6}{\sin 13}$

PS =
PR =

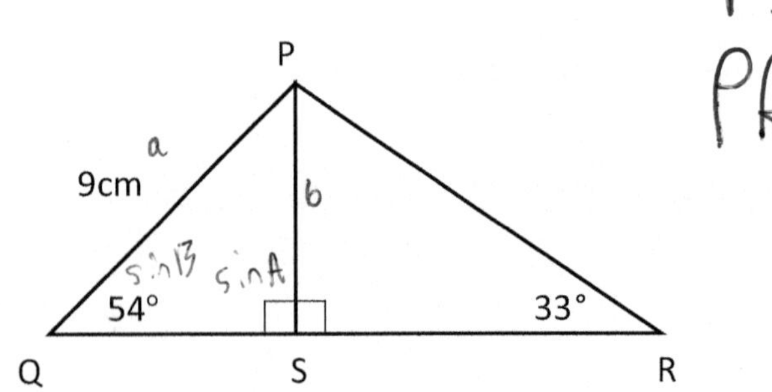

$6 = \frac{9}{\sin 90} \times \sin 54$

$6 =$

(4 marks)

5. Point A & B are such that A (2, -3) & B (6, 5)

$\frac{\text{Rise}}{\text{Run}} = \frac{8}{4} = 2$

(i) Work out equation of line AB.

$y = mx + c$

$y = 2x + c$

$5 = (2)(6) + c$

$5 = 12 + c$

$-7 = c$

$y = 2x - 7$

(2 marks)

(ii) Work out midpoint of line AB.

(4 , 1)

(1 mark)

(iii) Work out equation of perpendicular line to AB through midpoint.

$y = -\frac{1}{2} - 7$

(3 marks)

(total 6 marks)

6. A lorry was bought for £28,800 brand new. It decreases in value by 19% each year. Work out the value 3 years after it was bought.

19% of 28800 = 5472 (1st year) = 23328

14% of 23328 = £24367.68

3rd year = £24170.14

(3 marks)

7. Find x?

$$3^{x-1} \times 3^{2x} = 3^{x+7}$$

(3 marks)

8. A regular polygon has 15 sides.

   (i) Work out the sum of interior angles.

$(n-2) \times 180$

13×180

$= 2340°$

(3 marks)

   (ii) Work out an exterior angle.

$\frac{2340}{9} = 260$

$100°$

$360 - 260 = 100$

(1mark)

(total 4 marks)

9. Using your ruler and compass, construct a 60° angle in the space below.

(3 marks)

10. Solve the following equations

(i) $9x^2 - 49 = 0$

(3x + 7)(3x - 7)

(2 marks)

(ii)

$3x - 5y = 7$

$2x - 4y = 3$

(4 marks)

(total 6 marks)

11. The weights of some students are given below.

Weights (kg)	**Frequency**	**Frequency Density**
40-48	2	
48-54	9	
54-64	10	
64-69	7	
69-85	4	

Represent the above information on a histogram

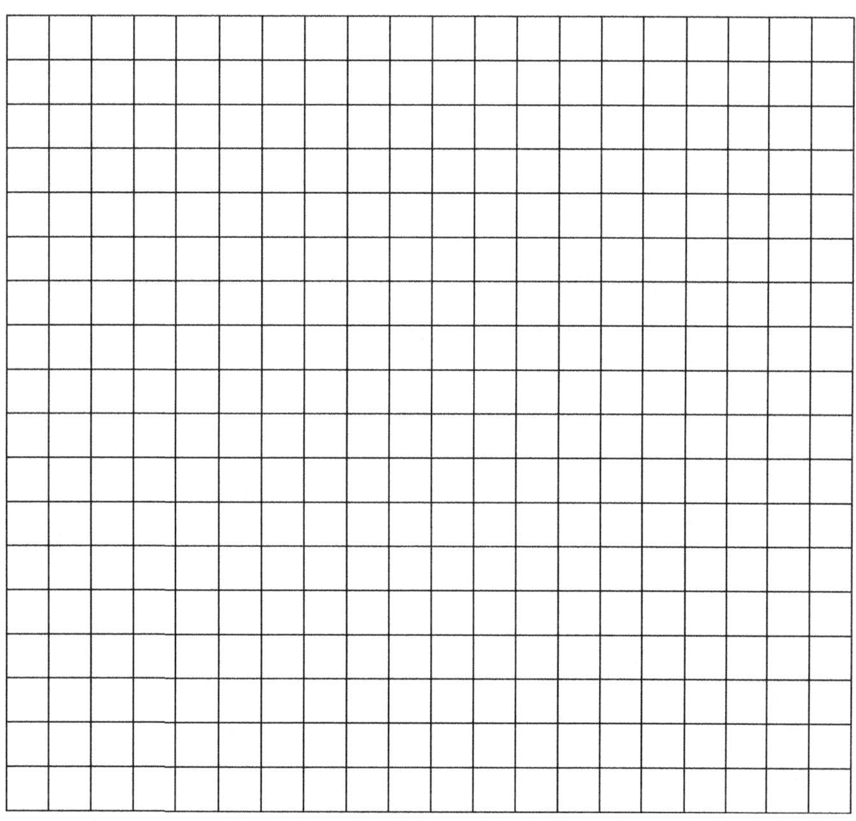

(4 marks)

12. $x^2 - 6x + 11 = (x - a)^2 + b$.

Find the values of a & b.

(3 marks)

13. Work out highest common factor and lowest common multiple of

(i) 96 and 120

(3 marks)

(ii) 210 and 350

(3 marks)

(total 6 marks)

14. A circle has a circumference of 35cm.

(i) Work out the radius of circle.

(2 marks)

(ii) Work out the area of circle.

(2 marks)

(total 4 marks)

15. Differentiate the following

(i) $y = x^3 - 3x^2 + 7x - 19$

(2 marks)

(ii) $y = (2x - 17)(3x + 4)$

(3 marks)

(total 5 marks)

16. A triangle ABC has sides AB = 4cm, BC = 7cm & AC = 9cm.
Calculate the area of triangle ABC.

(5 marks)

17. A school hall is to be tiled using tiles, which are 60cm x 40cm.
The hall is 50m x 50m. Each tile costs 68p and the tiler charges £85 per 100 square metres of tiling.
Calculate the total cost of tiling.

(5 marks)

18. Expand and simplify (x +1) (x – 3) (x +5)

(4 marks)

19.(a) Sketch the graph of $y = x^2 - 4x$ on the grid below, clearly showing the minimum point and all intersections with coordinate axes.

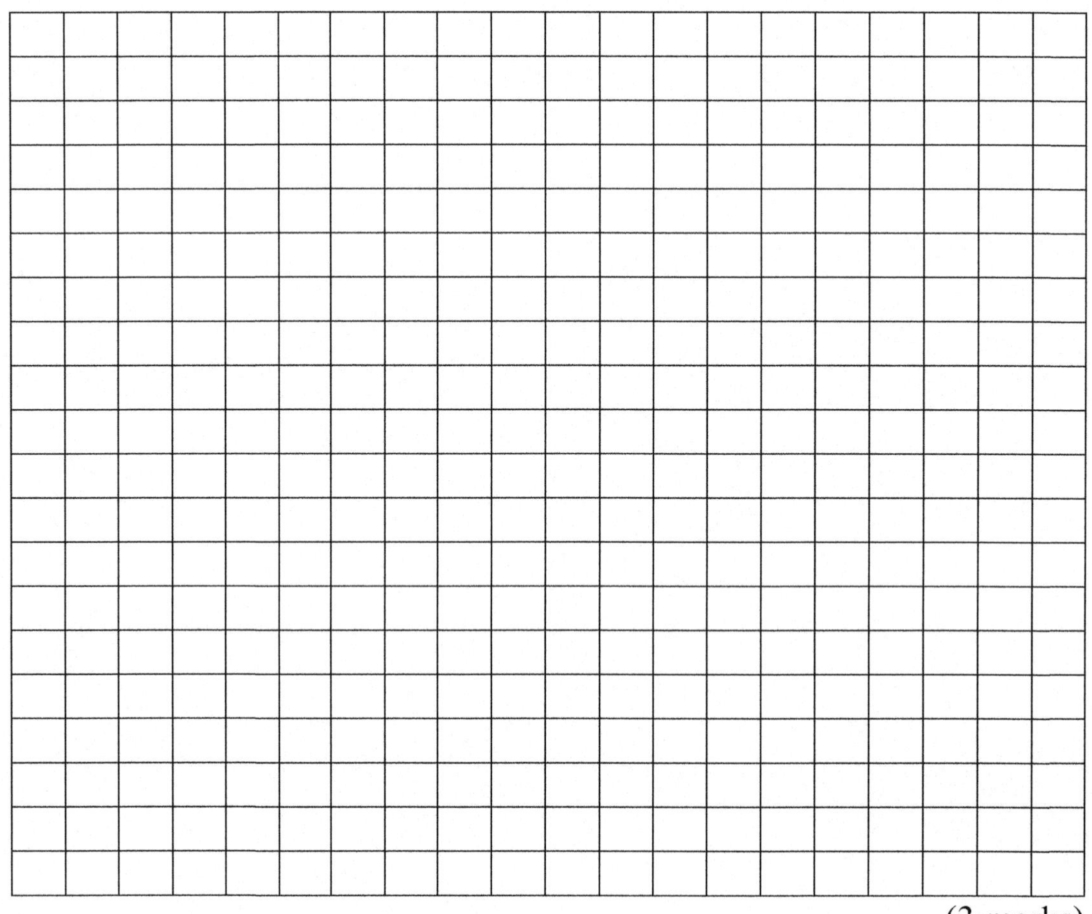

(3 marks)

(b) $f(x) = x^2 - 4x$. On the same grid, sketch

(i) $f(x - 3)$

(2 marks)

(ii) $2f(x)$

(1 mark)

(total 6 marks)

20. Simply the following

(i) $(5a^2b^{-3})^3$

(2 marks)

(ii) $\frac{2x^2-5x-12}{4x^2-9}$

(3 marks)

(iii) $\frac{3x-1}{x+5} - \frac{2x+3}{x-2}$

(3 marks)

(total 8 marks)

21. A sphere has the same surface area as a solid cylinder. The cylinder has a radius of 4cm and a height of 8cm.

(i) Work out the radius of the sphere.

(3 marks)

(ii) Hence work out the volume of the sphere.

(2 marks)

(iii) The radius of the sphere is correct to nearest cm. Work out maximum and minimum possible volumes for this sphere.

(3 marks)

(total 8 marks)

Total for paper: 100 marks

End

IGCSE Mathematics
Paper 2
(calculator)

Potential Paper D2

June 2021

You must have: Ruler graduated in centimetres and millimetres, protractor, pair of compasses, pen, HB pencil, eraser.

Calculator is allowed

Time allowed
2 hours
Total 100 marks

Write answers to 3 significant figures unless stated otherwise

1. Make x the subject of the formula.

$$y = \frac{5x - 1}{3x - 4}$$

(3 marks)

2. Liquid A has density $1.6gcm^{-3}$ and liquid B has density $2.4\ gcm^{-3}$.
100ml of A is mixed with 250ml of B. = 350ml
Work out the density of the mixture.

A = 1.6 g/cm^{-3} D = v/m

B = 2.4 g/cm^{-3}

4 g/m^{-3}

(4 marks)

3. Work out

i) $3\frac{1}{2} \div \left(2\frac{2}{3} - 1\frac{3}{4}\right)$

(3 marks)

ii) $\left(\frac{216}{343}\right)^{\frac{-1}{3}}$

(2 marks)
(total 5 marks)

4. The bearing of A from B is 078°.
Work out the bearing of B from A.

(3 marks)

5. A sphere has a surface area of $64\pi cm^2$.
   Work out its volume in terms of π

(3 marks)

6. A triangle ABC has coordinates A (1, 1), B (2, 3), C (1, 3)
   i) Plot the triangle ABC

(1 mark)

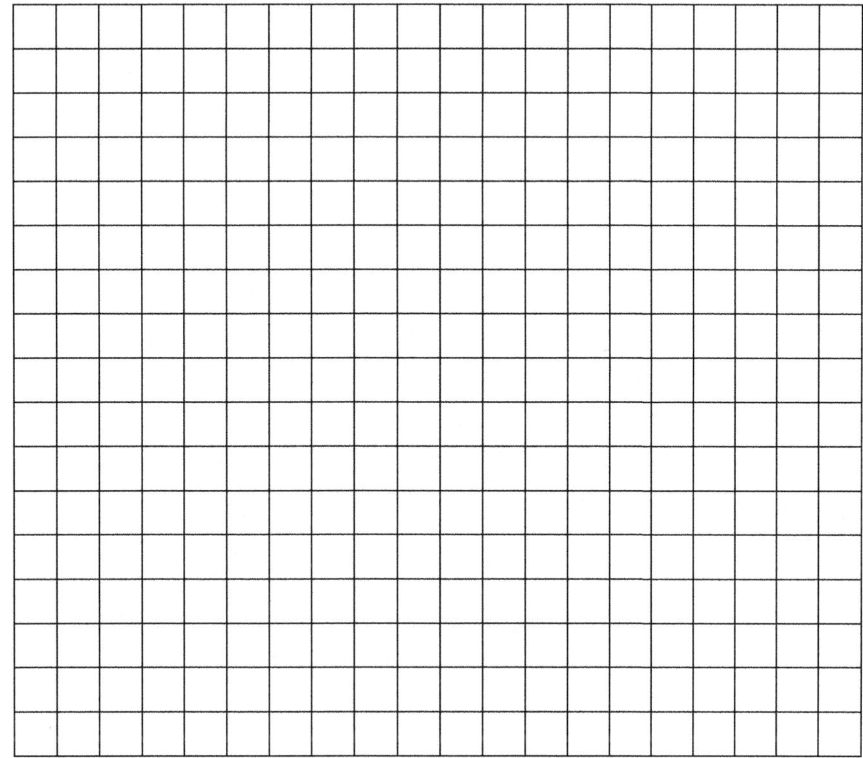

ii) Reflect triangle ABC on $y = x$ line.

(2 marks)

iii) Translate triangle ABC by $\begin{pmatrix} -4 \\ 1 \end{pmatrix}$

(2 marks)
(total 5 marks)

7. There are 6 red mangos and 5 green mangos in a bag.
   Andrew ate two mangos.
   i) Draw a tree diagram for all possibilities

(3 marks)

   ii) Work out probability of eating at least 1 red mango.

(3 marks)

(total 6 marks)

8. Work out the mean weight for information below

Weight(kg)	**Frequency**		
40-50	7		
50-60	11		
60-80	6		
80-100	2		

(3 marks)

9. There are 50 students in a sixth form. 28 of them study chemistry & 41 study mathematics. 2 of them do not study mathematics nor chemistry.

   i) Draw a Venn diagram for above information.

(2 marks)

   ii) Work out probability of a student studying both mathematics and chemistry.

(2 marks)

   iii) Work out probability of a student studying mathematics but not chemistry.

(2 marks)

(total 6 marks)

10.a. Factorise fully $64 - 49x^2$

(2 marks)

b. Expand and simplify $(2p - 3)(4p + 1)$

(2 marks)

c. Simplify fully $\frac{24a^2b^3 \times 49a^5b^7}{35a^{10}b^2 \times 18a^7b^3}$

(4 marks)

(8 marks)

11. Work out the following

i) The area of a circle, whose circumference is 25cm.

(3 marks)

ii) The area of a triangle, whose sides are 4cm, 7cm & 9cm.

(4 marks)

(total 7 marks)

12. (i) A house is worth £750,000. The value of the house increases by 8% each year. Work out the value in 10 years.

(2 marks)

(ii) A van is bought for £30,000 brand new. Its value depreciates by 18% each year. Find its value in 5 years.

(3 marks)

(total 5 marks)

13. Work out highest common factor and lowest common multiple of

i) 42 & 70

(3 marks)

ii) 96 & 160

(3 marks)

(6 marks)

14. $y = x^2 - 4x + 1$

i) Plot above graph for $-2 \leq x \leq 6$

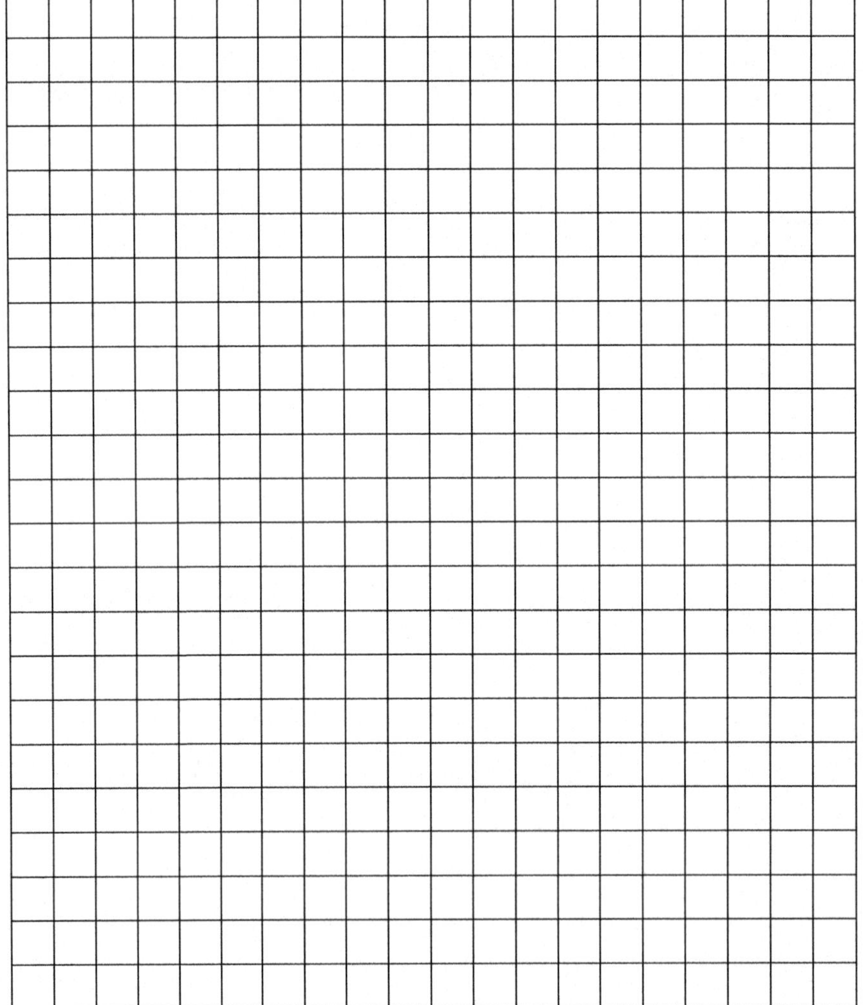

(2 marks)

ii) Using your graph solve

a. $x^2 - 4x + 1 = 0$

(2 marks)

b. $x^2 - 4x - 3 = 0$

(3 marks)

(7 marks)

15. A is inversely proportional to B. When A = 4, B = 5.

i) Find a formula for A in terms of B

(2 marks)

ii) Find A when B = 10

(2 marks)

iii) Find B when A = 15

(3 marks)
(total 7 marks)

16.

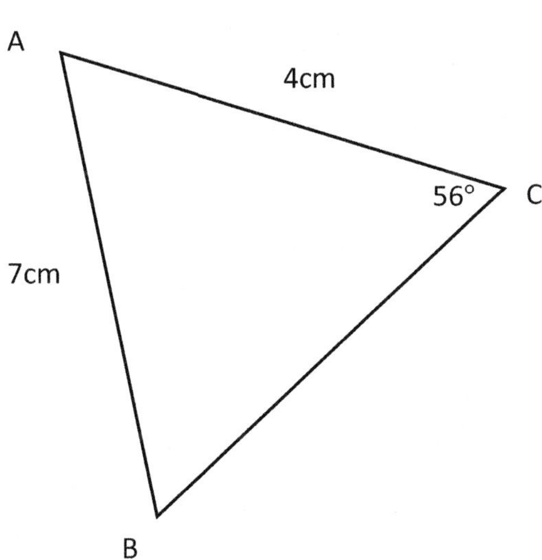

i) Find angle ABC

(2 marks)

ii) Hence, work out area of triangle ABC.

(3 marks)

(total 5 marks)

17. $y = 3x^2 - 5x + 1$

i) Find $\frac{dy}{dx}$ at $x = 2$

(3 marks)

ii) Hence or otherwise, find the equation of the tangent to curve at $x = 2$.

(4 marks)

(total 7 marks)

18. Rationalise the following

i) $\frac{15}{\sqrt{3}}$

(2 marks)

ii) $\frac{15-\sqrt{5}}{\sqrt{5}}$

(2 marks)

iii) $\frac{3}{3-\sqrt{2}}$

(2 marks)

(total 6 marks)

19. $2^{2x+1} \times 4^{x-1} = 8^{x/3}$

Find x

(4 marks)

Total for paper: 100 marks

End

Section E

IGCSE Mathematics
Paper 1
(calculator)

Potential Paper E1

May 2021

You must have: Ruler graduated in centimetres and millimetres, protractor, pair of compasses, pen, HB pencil, eraser.

Calculator is allowed

Time allowed
2 hours
Total 100 marks

Write answers to 3 significant figures unless stated otherwise

1. Data for some lengths are show in the table below

Lengths (cm)	**Frequency**		
20-40	3		
40-50	4		
50-80	6		
80-90	2		
90-120	1		

i) Write down the median class.

(1 mark)

ii) Work out the mean

(4 marks)

(total 5 marks)

2. Mary invested £5000 in a bank. The bank offers 4.5% compound interest annually. Work out her balance after 3 years.

(3 marks)

3. Solve the following equations

i) $\frac{5x-3}{2x+1} = \frac{3}{2}$

(3 marks)

ii) $5(3x-1) + 4(2x-5) = 11$

(3 marks)

(total 6 marks)

4. Joe and Mary shared 50 sweets in the ratio $7: x$. Joe had 20 more sweets than Mary. Find x?

(4 marks)

5. Write the following in standard form

i) 0.0734

(1 mark)

ii) 73400

(1 mark)

iii) $(7.3 \times 10^{-1}) \times (4 \times 10^{5})$

(2 marks)

(total 4 marks)

6. Work out the length BD.

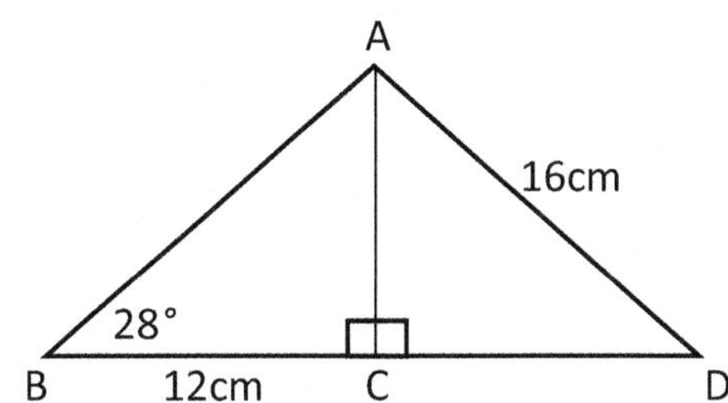

(5 marks)

7. Factorise fully

i) $64a^2 - 48a$

(1 mark)

ii) $64a^2 - 49$

(2 marks)

iii) $x^2 - 7x - 78$

(2 marks)

iv) $2x^2 - 25x + 50$

(3 marks)

(total 8 marks)

8. Find highest common factor and lowest common multiple of

   i) 30 and 48

(3 marks)

   ii) 84 and 140

(3 marks)

(total 6 marks)

9. AOB is a sector of a circle. Work out the area of the shaded region.

   AB = 6cm & OB = 10cm

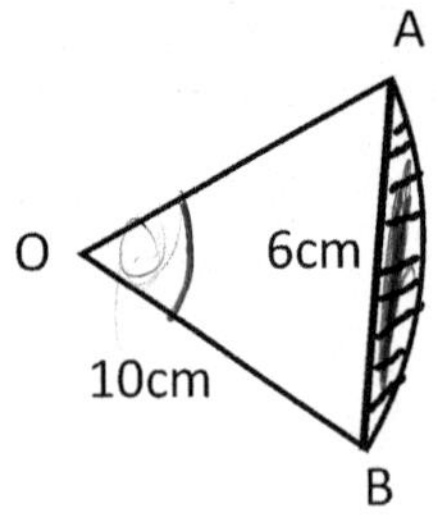

(5 marks)

10. A company's salary structure for 24 people are shown below.

Salary (£)	Frequency	Cumulative Frequency
1000-2000	5	
2000-4000	8	
4000-8000	7	
8000-10000	3	
10000-15000	1	

i) Draw a cumulative frequency curve

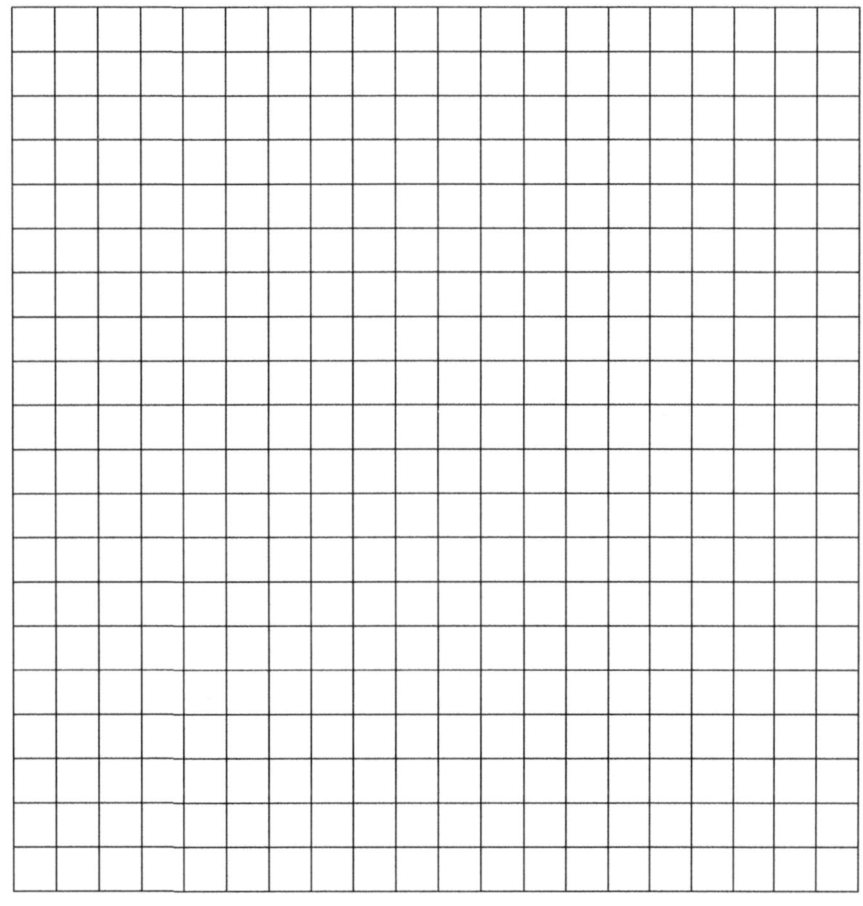

(2 marks)

ii) Work out median salary

(1 mark)

iii) Work out the interquartile range

(3 marks)
(total 6 marks)

11.a) Expand $(x-3)^3$

(3 marks)

b) Solve the following

$$xy = 15$$
$$y - x = 2$$

(3 marks)
(total 6 marks)

12.Solve the following inequalities

i) $3x - 2 \geq 7$

(2 marks)

ii) $x^2 - 5x - 6 < 0$

(4 marks)
(total 6 marks)

13. Angle OAB is 28°, ACD is a straight line & O is the centre of the circle. Work out the angle BCD. (write reasons for each stage of your working)

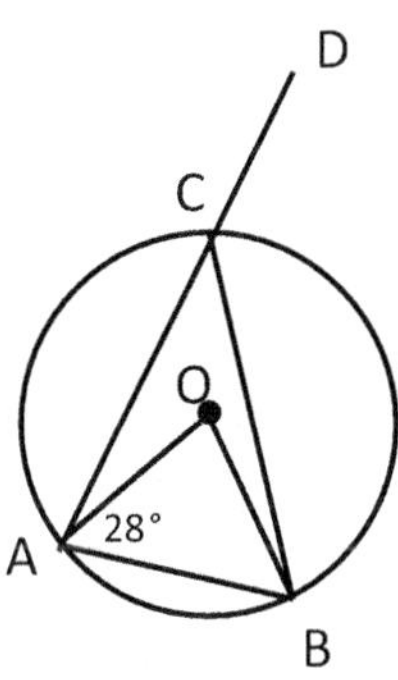

(4 marks)

14. $f(x) = 2x - 3$ & $g(x) = x^2$

i) Work out $fg(x)$

(2 marks)

ii) Find $f^{-1}(x)$

(2 marks)

iii) Find $gf(-3)$

(2 marks)
(total 6 marks)

15.Simplify fully

i) $(2x^3y^6)^2 \times (3x^2y^3)^3$

(3 marks)

ii) $\left(\frac{64a^3}{125b^9}\right)^{\frac{2}{3}}$

(3 marks)

(total 6 marks)

16.A cylinder has a radius of 4cm and a height of 18cm. The cylinder is melted down and made into a sphere.

i) Work out the radius of the sphere.

(4 marks)

ii) Hence, work out the surface area of the sphere.

(2 marks)

(total 6 marks)

17. $\overrightarrow{OB} = b, \overrightarrow{OC} = c$ & $BD: DC = 3: 2$

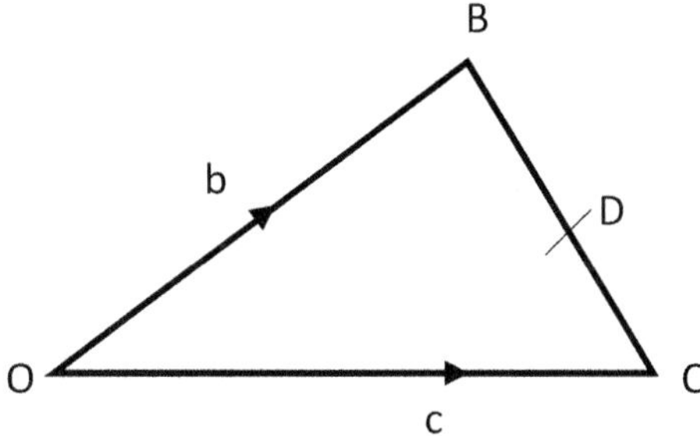

i) Work out $\overrightarrow{BC}$

(2 marks)

ii) Hence or otherwise, work out $\overrightarrow{OD}$

(3 marks)
(total 5 marks)

18. Points A & B are such that A (1, -3), B (4, 2).
Work out the equation of line AB.

(4 marks)

19. $y = f(x)$ is sketched below.
Where A (0, 0), B (2, 2), C (4, 0)

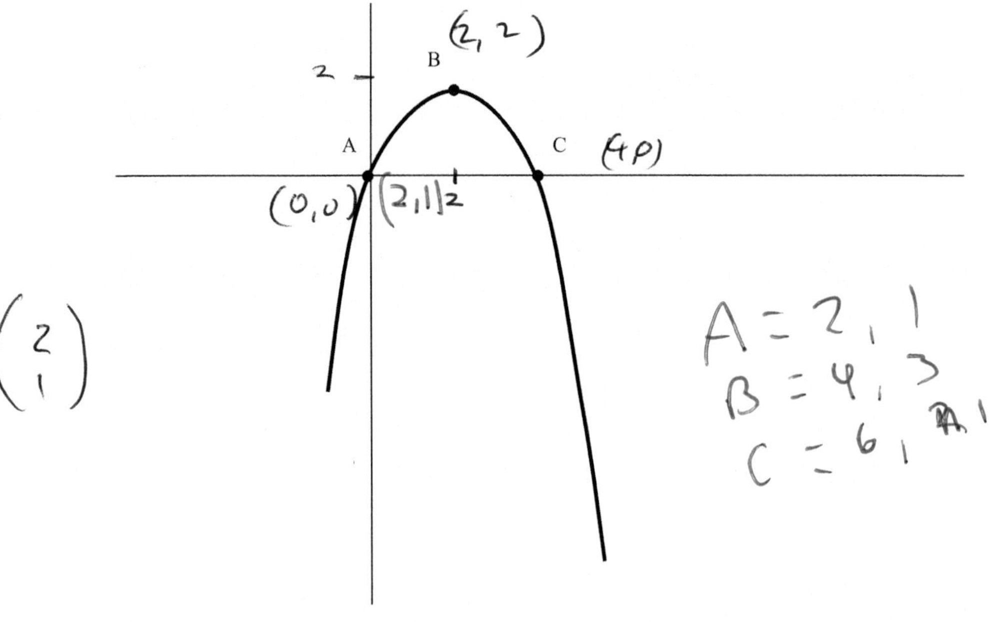

i) Sketch $y = f(x - 2) + 1$

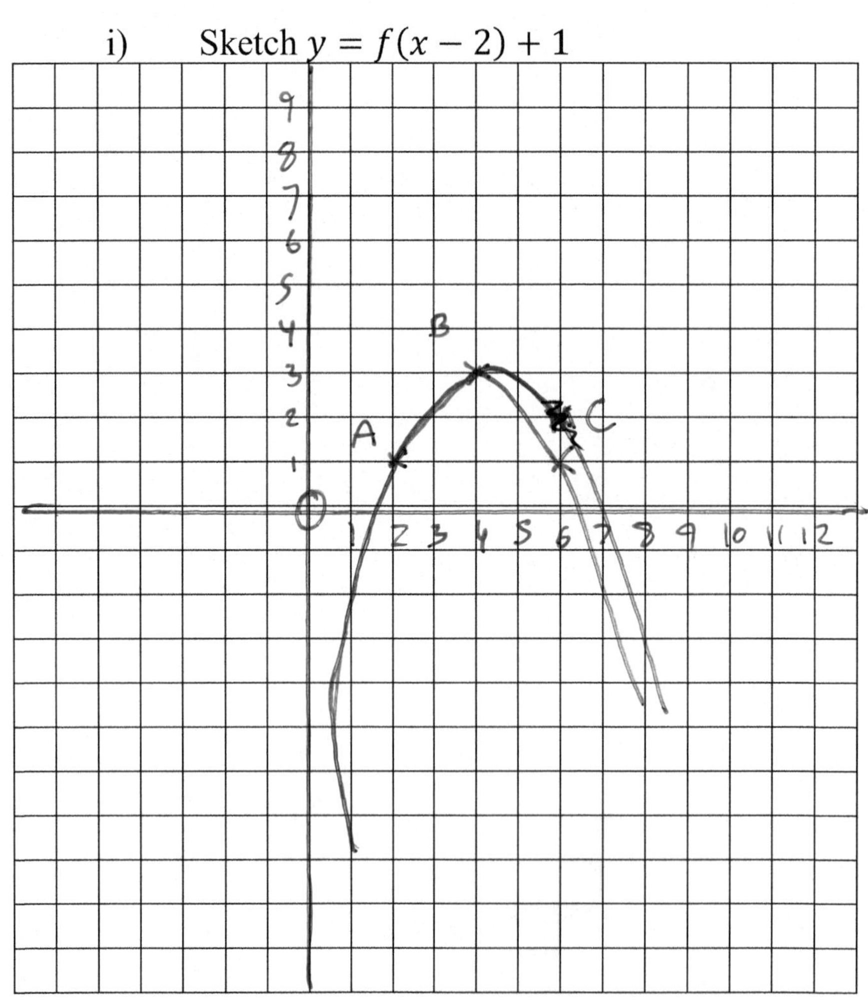

(2 marks)

ii) Sketch $y = 2f(x + 4) - 3$

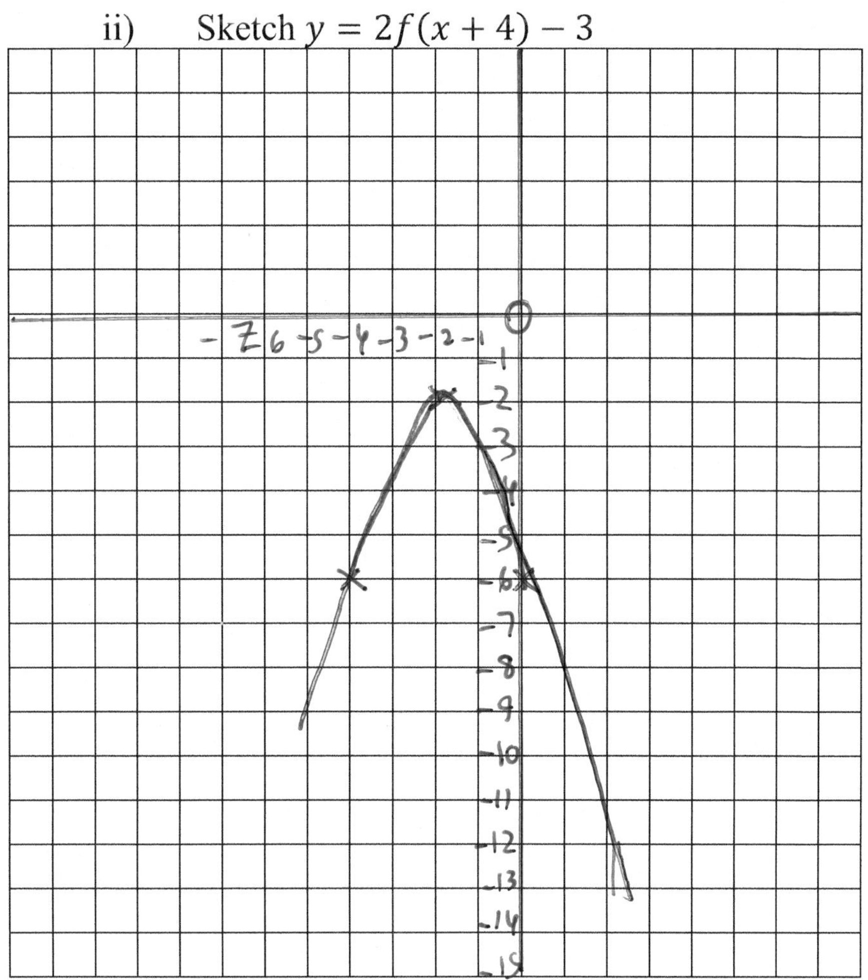

(3 marks)
(total 5 marks)

Total for paper: 100 marks

End

IGCSE Mathematics
Paper 2
(calculator)

Potential Paper E2

June 2021

You must have: Ruler graduated in centimetres and millimetres, protractor, pair of compasses, pen, HB pencil, eraser.

Calculator is allowed

Time allowed
2 hours
Total 100 marks

Write answers to 3 significant figures unless stated otherwise

1. Expand and simplify

$$(2 - 3\sqrt{2})(5 + \sqrt{2})$$

$10 - 2\sqrt{2} - 15\sqrt{2} - 6$

$10 - 17\sqrt{2} - 6$

$16 - 17\sqrt{2}$

(3 marks)

2. $y = \sqrt{2x^2 - 9}$
   Make x the subject of the formula.

$y^2 = 2x^2 - 9$

$y^2 + 9 = 2x^2$

$\sqrt{\frac{y^2+9}{2}} = x$

(3 marks)

3. Solve the following equations

i) $\frac{3a-5}{2a+7} = \frac{1}{2}$

$a = 4.25$

$2(3a-5) = 2a + 7$

$6a - 10 = 2a + 7$

$6a - 2a = 17$

$4a = 17$

$a = \frac{17}{4}$

(3 marks)

ii) $5x - 4y = 7$
$3x - 7y = -5$

$15x - 12y = 21$

$15x - 35y = -25$

$23y = -46$

$y = -\frac{46}{23}$

$y = -2$

$3x - 7(-2) = -5$

$3x - 14 = -5$

$3x = 9$

$x = 3$

$x = 3 \quad y = -2$

(4 marks)
(total 7 marks)

4. Points A & B are such that A (2, -3), B (6, 0)
   i) Find midpoint of AB

(1 mark)

   ii) Find gradient of line AB

(2 marks)

   iii) Find distance AB

(3 marks)
(total 6 marks)

5. Write the following as fractions
   i) $0.1\dot{7}$

(2 marks)

   ii) $0.\dot{1}\dot{7}$

(2 marks)

   iii) $0.0\dot{1}\dot{7}$

(3 marks)
(total 7 marks)

6. Work out QR

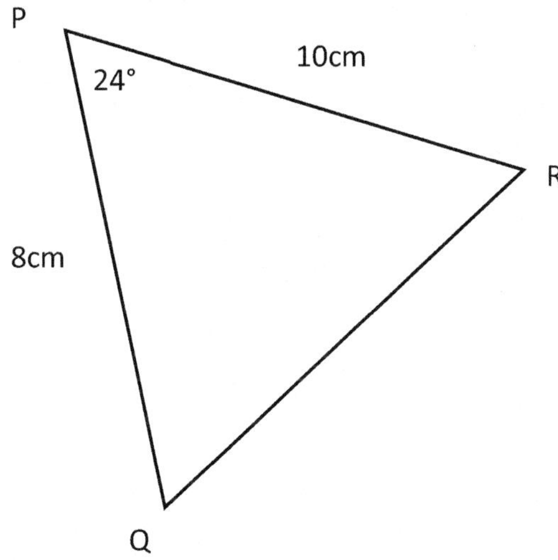

(3 marks)

7. $a = 7, b = -2, c = -1$
Work out the following
i) $5a - b$

(2 marks)

ii) $a^2 - 3b - 4c$

(4 marks)
(total 6 marks)

8.

i) A car is bought for £18,000. It depreciates in value by 22% each year. Find its value in 4 years.

(2 marks)

ii) A land is valued at £95,000 this year. It is expected to increase in value by 6% each year. Find its value in 15 years.

(2 marks)
(total 4 marks)

9. A cuboid has length 9cm, width 6cm & height 4cm. The cuboid is melted down and is made into a cube. Work out the surface area of the cube?

(5 marks)

10. Work out areas of the following shapes.

i) A circle, whose circumference is 36cm.

(3 marks)

ii) A right-angled triangle, whose hypotenuse is 13cm and the base side is 5cm.

(3 marks)
(total 6 marks)

11. An arithmetic sequence has first term 5 and a common difference 4.
Work out

i) 23rd term

(3 marks)

ii) Sum of first 86 terms

(3 marks)
(total 6 marks)

12. $2x^2 - 16x + 1 = a(x - b)^2 + c$
Find a, b & c.

(4 marks)

13. Solve the following equations

i) $25x^2 - 9 = 0$

$(5x - 3)(5x + 3)$

(2 marks)

ii) $x^2 - 23x + 120 = 0$

(3 marks)

iii) $8x^2 - 13x - 6 = 0$

(3 marks)
(total 8 marks)

14. Find a & b.

$$\frac{2}{x-3} + \frac{3}{x+3} = \frac{ax+b}{x^2-9}$$

(4 marks)

15. P is inversely proportional to Q^2 and when $P = 3, Q = 6$.
Find Q when $P = 12$.

(4 marks)

16. A regular polygon has 15 sides.
Work out the value of each interior angle.

(3 marks)

17. A curve has equation $y = 3x^3 - 5x + \frac{2}{x^2}$

i) Find $\frac{dy}{dx}$

(3 marks)

ii) Work out the gradient of curve at $x = 1$

(3 marks)
(total 6 marks)

18. Solve $2x^2 - 8x + 7 = 0$
(write your answers to 3 significant figures)

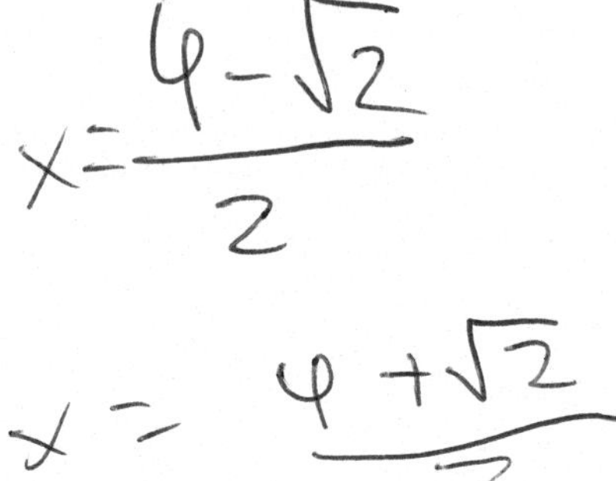

(4 marks)

19. A church hall is 70m long and 30m wide. The hall is to be tiled using tiles, which are 65cm by 50cm. Each tile costs 72 pence and the tiler charges £78 per $150m^2$ area of tiling.
Calculate the total cost of tiling.

(5 marks)

20. Data for some weights are shown in the table below.

Weight(g)	Frequency	Class Width	Frequency Density
20-30	2		
30-35	6		
35-50	15		
50-70	4		
70-100	3		

i) Draw a histogram for the above data

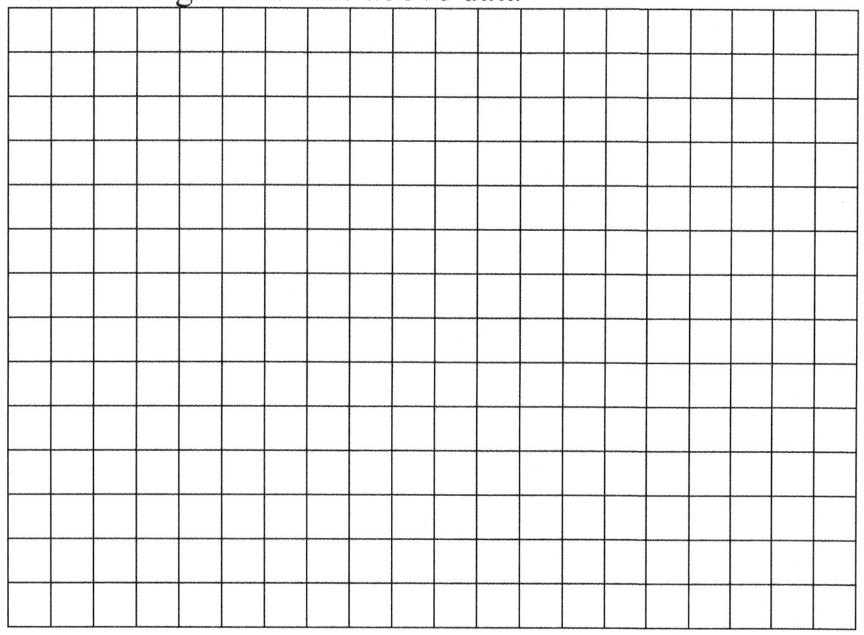

(3 marks)

ii) Calculate the percentage of weights over 65g

(3 marks)
(total 6 marks)

Total for paper: 100 marks

End

Answers

Paper A1	Paper A2
1.$i)$ $(6,-1), ii) \frac{1}{2}, iii)\ y = -2x + 1$	1.$i)$ $28a^3b^{14}c^4, ii) \frac{8x^{15}}{27y^6}$
2. $360 = 2 \times 2 \times 2 \times 3 \times 3 \times 5$	2.$i)2{,}500{,}000{,}000m^3, ii)0.0046cm^3$
3. $153.94cm^2$	3. Correct Proof
4.$i)$ $26, ii)\ 70, iii)\ correct\ box\ plot$	4.$i)$ $32.6°, ii)\ 54.6°$
5.$\frac{3}{10}$	5.correct construction with evidence.
6. 2.812×10^3	6.$i)$ $correct\ tree\ diagram, ii) \frac{5}{7}$
7.$a) 2x^3 + x^2 - 18x - 9, b)\ 3x(x+4)(x-4)$	7.$i) x < -1, x > 1, ii)\ x = 2 \pm \sqrt{3}$
8. $i\ \&\ ii\ correct\ plots$	8. Year 2 with evidence.
9. $44.68cm^2$	9.$i)$ $64km/h, ii)\ 17.8m/s$
10. No, Max is wrong.	10. $47.71cm^3$
11. Correct region must be shaded after sketching.	11. France is better value.
12. $0.4cm^3$	12. Correct proof using a diagram.
13. Correct histogram.	13. Correct sketch.
14. 44.9°	14. $\frac{1}{4}$
15. $3\pi x^3 cm^3$	15. $a = \sqrt{\frac{b^2-1}{5b^2-2}}$
16. 12.494	16. Correct proof.
17. $a = 5, b = 2.$	17.$i)$ $Correct\ curve, ii)\ 332, iii)\ 45, iv)\ 13$
18.$i)$ $\frac{dy}{dx} = 8x - 3, ii) - 11, iii)\ x = 3/8$	18. $x = \frac{1+3\sqrt{5}}{2}$
19. $47.01cm^2$	19.$\frac{(2x-3)(x-4)}{(x+3)(x-5)}$
20. Correct sketches.	20.Correct sketch through $(1,1)$& $(3,3)$.
21.$i)$ $\frac{3x+2}{3x-1}, ii)\ f^{-1}(x) = \frac{x+3}{x-1}$	21.$i)$ $x = -1, y = 1,$ $ii)\ When\ x = 2, y = 7\ \&$ $when\ x = -\frac{13}{5}, y = -\frac{34}{5}$
22. $\frac{1}{4}(3b - a)$	
23. $x = 6, y = 13$	

Paper B1	Paper B2
1. $x = 2$	1. £379.03
2. 56.55g	2. construction shown
3. $i)\ (3x+5)(3x-5)$ $ii)\ (2x-3)(2x+1)$ $iii)\ (a+3b)(a+3b)$	3. $\frac{1}{3}$
4. 10	4. $x = 6.45cm$
5. proof shown	5. 20%
6. 25km	6. 3.14cm
7. $i)\ 27x^{15}y^{12}$ $ii)\ x^2 - 8x + 4$	7. 33.3m/s
8. plots shown	8. ~~12~~ 30
9. $\frac{1}{9}$	9. $x = 5, y = 6$ $(x = -6, y = -5)$
10. $i)\ 2.34 \times 10^{-3}$ $ii)\ 3.5\ \times 10^{-4}$ $iii)\ 23400$	10. $i)\ mid\ point\ (1,3)$ $ii)\ y = 2x + 3$
11. £3542.40	11. £850
12. $13.02cm^2$	12. 26.63cm
13. $HCF = 40, LCM = 840$	13. $\frac{4}{6}b - \frac{1}{6}a$
14. $i)\ 254.47cm^2, ii)\ 179.59cm^3$	14. $i)\ cumulative\ frequency\ curve\ drawn$ $ii)\ median = 58g, iii) I.Q.R. = 39g, iv)\ 20.8\%$
15. $a = 6, b = -29$	15. $i)\ x = \frac{2y^2-5}{y^2-3}, ii)\ 3$
16. proof shown	16. $p = 13, q = -8$
17. a) Venn diagram drawn b) $\frac{1}{10}$	17. $B = \pm 5$
18. 1100	18. $\frac{dy}{dx} = 1$
19. PQ = 12cm, RT = 3cm	19. $166.73cm^2$
20. $19.73cm^2$	20. $i)\ x > \frac{9}{4}, ii) -\frac{1}{2} < x < 2\ with\ a\ sketch$
21. proof shown	21. $i)\ 2x^2 + 3, ii) \frac{x-5}{2}, iii)\ 80$
22. histogram drawn	22. $i)\ 2.45cm, ii)\ 130.06cm^2$
23. angles $CBD = 56°,\ ABD = 34°, ACD = 34°,$ $BDC = 34°$	
24. sketch shown	
25. $i)\ r = 4.9cm, ii)\ A = 520.31cm^2$	

Paper C1	Paper C2
1. $i)\ 3x^2(2x-1),\ ii)\ (5y+4x)(5y-4x)$ $iii)\ (x-2)(x-1), iv)\ (5x-2)(x+3)$	1. $HCF = 24, LCM = 288$
2. $i)\ HCF = 14, LCM = 210$ $ii)\ HCF = 48, LCM = 288$	2. $i) -4n+37, ii)\ no\ with\ proof$
3. $i)\ fg(x) = 3x^2-5, ii)\ 64, iii)\ \frac{x+5}{3}$	3. $r = 3cm$
4. £570	4. $x = \frac{29}{4}$
5. $i)\ C = 47.1cm, ii)\ 18.1cm$	5. £800
6. AD = 9.8cm, AC = 12.65cm	6. $41.0cm^2$
7. $a)i)2.037\times10^3, ii)2.307\times10^1, iii)2.37\times10^{-2}$ $b)\ i)\ 0.002037, ii)230.7, iii)50$	7. $i) -11, ii)\ 31$
8. $y = \frac{2-5ax^2}{3}$	8. 1.748
9. $3\frac{7}{11}$	9. $i)\ (3y+7)(3y-7), ii)\ (x-15)(x+3)$ $iii)\ (x-4)(3x-5)$
10. $280.33cm^3$	10. $i)\frac{7}{20}, ii)\frac{7}{25}, iii)\frac{13}{45}$
11. $i)\ 12.71cm, ii)\ 12.21cm, iii)\ 12.54cm^2$	11. $i)\ r = 17.8cm, ii)\ 71.9cm^2$
12. $i)\ cumulative\ frequency\ curve\ drawn$ $ii)\ median$ £2200, $iii)\ I.Q.R.=$ £800	12. $23.5cm^2$
13. $i)\ x^2-22x+2, ii)\ 3x^2-13x+15$	13. $i)\ 27a^6b^{-9}, ii)\ 3x^2-2x+4$
14. 65km/h	14. $x = \sqrt{\frac{a^2+b}{2}}$
15. $5.86g/cm^3$	15. $i)\ x \le \frac{2}{3}, ii)\ x < 4\ \&\ x > 6\ with\ a\ sketch$
16. $-1 \le x < 5\ with\ the\ number\ line\ shown$	16. $midpoint\ (5,8), ii)\ y = \frac{3}{2}x + \frac{1}{2}$
17. $i)\frac{1}{8}, ii)\ \pm\frac{1}{\sqrt{5}}$	17. $i)tree\ diagran\ drawn, ii)\frac{4}{7}, iii)\frac{6}{7}$
18. $x = 3, y = 5$	18. $i)\ \frac{dy}{dx} = 2x-5, ii)\ y = x-6$
	19. $i)\ x = 3, y = 2, ii)\ x = 3, y = 7$
	20. $a)\ i)\ 2\sqrt{2}-1,\ ii)\ 6\sqrt{3}$ $b)\ i)\ 6\sqrt{2},\ ii)\ 5\sqrt{3}-1$

Paper D1	**Paper D2**
1. i) a = 5, ii) 230	1. $x = \frac{4y-1}{3y-5}$
2. £210	2. 2.17g/cm^3
3.£37.77	3. $i)\ 3\frac{9}{11}, ii)\ \frac{7}{6}$
4. PS = 7.28cm, PR = 13.67cm	4. 258°
5. $i) y = 2x - 7, ii)\ midpoint\ (4,1), iii)\ y = \frac{1}{2}x - 1$	5. $\frac{256}{3}\pi cm^3$
6. £14880.35	6. Plots and sketches shown
7. $x = 4$	7. i) tree diagram shown, ii) $\frac{9}{11}$
8. $i)\ 2340°, ii)\ 24°$	8. 58.5kg
9. construction drawn	9. i) Venn diagram shown, ii) $\frac{21}{50}$, iii) $\frac{2}{5}$
10. $i)\ x = -\frac{7}{3}\ or \frac{7}{3}, ii)\ x = 6.5\ \&\ y = 2.5$	10. $a)\ (8 + 7x)(8 - 7x), b)\ 8p^2 - 10p - 3$ c) $\frac{28b^5}{15a^{10}}$
11. histogram drawn	11. i) 49.8cm^2, ii) 13.42cm^2
12. a = 3, b = 2	12. $i)$ £1,619,193.75, $ii)$ £11,122.20
13. $i) HCF = 24, LCM = 480, ii) HCF\ 70, LCM 1050$	13. $i)\ HCF = 14, LCM = 210,$ $ii)\ HCF = 32, LCM = 480$
14. $i)\ r = 5.57cm, ii)\ 97.47cm^2$	14. i) plot shown, ii) solve using the plot
15. $\frac{dy}{dx} = 3x^2 - 6x + 7, ii)\ \frac{dy}{dx} = 12x - 43$	15. i) A = 2, ii) B= $\frac{4}{3}$
16. 13.42cm^2	16. $i)\ 28.3°, ii)\ 13.93cm^2$
17. £9208.56	17. $i) \frac{dy}{dx} = 1, ii)\ y = x + 1$
18 $x^3 + 3x^2 - 13x - 15$	18. $i)\ 5\sqrt{3}, ii)\ 3\sqrt{5} - 1, iii)\ 9 + 3\sqrt{2}$
19. sketches shown	19. $x = \frac{1}{3}$
20. $i)\ 125a^6b^{-9}, ii)\ \frac{x-4}{x2x-3}, iii)\ \frac{x^2-20x-13}{x^2+3x-10}$	
21. $i)\ r = 4.9cm, ii)\ 492.81cm^3$ iii) min 381.7cm^3& max 696.9cm^3	

Paper E1	Paper E2
1. i) median 50-80, ii) 58.4cm	1. $4 - 13\sqrt{2}$
2. £5705.83	2. $x = \sqrt{\frac{y^2+9}{2}}$
3. $i)\ x = \frac{9}{4}, ii)\ x = \frac{36}{23}$	3. $i)\ a = \frac{17}{4}, ii)\ y = 2$
4. $x = 3$	4. $i)\ \left(4, -\frac{3}{2}\right), ii)\ \frac{3}{4}, iii)\ 5$
5. $i)\ 7.34 \times 10^{-2}, ii)\ 7.34 \times 10^4, iii)\ 2.92 \times 10^5$	5. $i)\ \frac{8}{45}, ii)\ \frac{17}{99}, iii)\ \frac{17}{990}$
6. 26.7cm	6. QR = 4.22cm
7. $i)\ 16a(4a - 3), ii)\ (8a + 7)(8a - 7)$ $iii)\ (x - 13)(x + 6), iv)\ (x - 10)(2x - 5)$	7. $i)\ 37, ii)\ 59$
8. $i) HCF = 6, LCM = 120$ $ii)\ HCF = 28, LCM = 420$	8. $i)$ £6662.71, $ii)$ £227673.03
9. $1.85cm^2$	9. $216cm^2$
10. i) median = £3700, ii) I.Q.R. = £2400	10. $i)\ 103.15cm^2, ii)\ 30cm^2$
11. $x^3 - 9x^2 + 27x - 27$	11. $i)\ 93, ii)\ 15050$
12. $i)\ x \geq 3, ii) - 1 < x < 6$ *with a sketch*	12. $a = 2, b = 4, c = -31$
13. 118°	13. $i)\ x = -\frac{3}{5}$ *or* $\frac{3}{5}, ii)\ x = 15$ *or* $x = 8$ $iii)\ x = 2$ *or* $x = -\frac{3}{8}$
14. $i)\ 2x^2 - 3, ii)\ \frac{x+3}{2}$	14. $a = 5, b = -3$
15. $i)\ 108x^{12}\ y^{21}, ii) \frac{16a^2}{25b^6}$	15. $Q = \pm 3$
16. $i)\ r = 6cm, ii)\ 144\pi cm^2$	16. 156°
17. $i)\ c - b, ii)\ \frac{2}{5}b + \frac{3}{5}c$	17. $i)\ \frac{dy}{dx} = 9x^2 - 5 - 4x^{-3}, ii)\ \frac{dy}{dx} = 0$
18. $y = \frac{5}{3}x - \frac{14}{3}$	18. $x = 2.71$ *or* $x = 1.29$
19. sketches shown	19. £5744.64
	20. i) histogram shown, ii) 13.3%

Printed in Great Britain
by Amazon